Brunel's Big Railway

CREATION OF THE GREAT WESTERN RAILWAY

BRUNEL'S
BIG RAILWAY
Creation of the Great Western Railway

ROBIN JONES

First published as Brunel's Big Railway in 2013
by Mortons Media Group

This edition published in 2021 by Gresley Books,
an imprint of Mortons Books Ltd.
Media Centre
Morton Way
Horncastle LN9 6JR
www.mortonsbooks.co.uk

ISBN 978-1-911658-19-1

The right of Robin Jones to be identified as the author of this work has been
asserted in accordance with the Copyright, Designs and Patents Act 1988.

Typeset by Jayne Clements (jayne@hinoki.co.uk), Hinoki Design and Typesetting.
Printed and bound by Gutenberg Press, Malta.

10 9 8 7 6 5 4 3 2 1

In memory of Mowgli.
Our wonderful roaming marble Bengal station cat

Contents

Introduction

FOR THE first half of the 20th century, the Great Western Railway, otherwise known as God's Wonderful Railway, stood high above the rest as an international byword for excellence in the field of transport technology. Those were the halcyon days when Stars, Castles and Kings either set the world alight or filled it with steam and smoke aplenty.

The sight of Brunswick green-liveried engines big and small hauling chocolate and cream-liveried coaches or long rakes of wagons was a mark of prestige for Britain. The company's 'Cheltenham Spa Express' was the fastest train in the world, before the mighty London & North Eastern Railway's glamorous streamlined A4 Pacifics made their debut on the East Coast Main Line.

From the chairman, board of directors and chief mechanical engineers down to the ticket collector and station porter, the Paddington and Swindon empire was an immense source of pride to everyone who worked for it. The great railway to the west took millions of people to summer holiday destinations and inspired schoolboys who watched awestruck as the immaculately turned-out locomotives thundered down the lines.

The Great Western. It was exactly what the name says, and will always be remembered as such. Magnificent though the locomotive designs of George Jackson Churchward and Charles Benjamin Collett were however, they merely superseded what in many ways was an equally great and arguably more ground-breaking railway, the like of which Britain had never seen before. The Great Western Railway — 'first time round'.

Born out of a desire and indeed desperation to maintain the economy of Bristol — one of the most important ports in Britain which had made much of its wealth on the by-then outlawed slave trade — plans were made to emulate the success of the Liverpool & Manchester Railway and link the city to London.

And the man appointed to do the job was a little-known workaholic young engineer called Isambard Kingdom Brunel.

Aged just 27, he had the audacity to tear up the rule book and lead the Great Western Railway into the deepest of uncharted waters; designing bridges and tunnels which those who 'knew better' said could never be built.

From day one, he not only proved them wrong but also imbued his buildings and infrastructure with the features of classical architecture, uniquely improving the cities, towns and landscapes through which his railway ran. Never mind the budget: Brunel was a visionary and he was going to have the best.

Daniel Gooch, the young locomotive engineer who made Brunel's railway 'happen' by designing superior engines to run over it, would later remark on the passing of his former mentor: "By his death the greatest of England's engineers was lost, the man with the greatest originality of thought and power of execution, bold in his plans but right. The commercial world thought him extravagant; but although he was so, great things are not done by those who sit down and count the cost of every thought and act."

Defying convention, Isambard Brunel cast aside established steam railway practice, started with a blank sheet of paper and designed a railway from scratch which would be better than any other. It had to be faster, and capable of carrying the biggest payloads.

The end result: the Great Western's 7ft ¼in broad gauge, Brunel's Big Railway… one which was destined to carry passengers and freight not just from Paddington to Bristol, but also across the Atlantic Ocean to New York and, nearer to home, via Exeter and Plymouth to Penzance.

This was the age of oversize engines with gleaming copper steam domes, stovepipe chimneys, wooden boiler cladding, no protection from wind, rain, snow or summer heat for the driver and firemen and, to begin with, third class passengers travelling in open wagons.

It was also the subject of great controversy throughout much of the reign of Queen Victoria. Even though they set several world speed records, and the locomotives proved in trials that they were superior, broad gauge trains could not run on to the standard gauge to which most of the rest of Britain's network was built, and passengers had to change trains where the two met, with freight, by necessity, being loaded and offloaded again.

Eventually one size had to fit all and, despite its many advantages and arguably superior technology, Brunel's Big Railway had to go.

Just as broad gauge finally conceded defeat to standard gauge in 1892, so Great Western steam was replaced by diesel haulage in the late Fifties and Sixties. Now the time had come for another great transitional period on the first main line that Brunel built, and one of which I have no doubt he would have approved – electrification.

On March 1, 2011, the green light was given for the Great Western Main Line to be electrified all the way from London to Bristol and beyond to Cardiff, a package costing nearly £1 billion, with a new fleet of high-speed trains brought in.

Brunel's railway would receive the benefits enjoyed by the West Coast Main Line from London to Glasgow in the Sixties, when it was electrified, much of that project taking place at the same time as British Railways chairman Dr Richard Beeching was implementing his cuts elsewhere. Rail travel on the route was made more attractive, with journey times especially for commuters and overcrowding cut, and the same is now expected to happen on the Great Western Main Line.

Hitachi was announced as the preferred bidder for providing 533 new carriages, with 308 for use on the Great Western Main Line. The 'bi-mode' trains, able to run on both electric and diesel lines, replaced the ageing though successful fleet of Class 125 High Speed Trains.

In 2009, when the previous Labour government had announced its intention to have the route similarly upgraded by 2017, the only electrified stretch lay between London Paddington and Airport Junction, with a 25kV AC overhead system for the Heathrow Express service. This electrification will be extended from Airport Junction to Maidenhead under the separate Crossrail scheme.

In November 2010, Transport Secretary Philip Hammond gave the go-ahead for the line from Oxford via Didcot and Newbury to London to be electrified within six years. Four months later, he announced that rail electrification from Didcot Parkway to Bristol Temple Meads and Cardiff Central would go ahead. The section linking Bristol Parkway and Bristol Temple Meads would also be electrified, he stated.

In March 2012, Amey plc announced that it had been awarded a £700 million contract to undertake the electrification works, and in July that year the Coalition government announced that the final portion of the Great Western from Cardiff to Swansea would also be electrified.

Meanwhile, other major improvements to Brunel's Big Railway had already begun.

Back in September 2008, Network Rail had unveiled a £400 million regeneration and reconfiguration of Reading station, creating an overpass to the west of the station so that passenger and freight trains could switch from the fast Reading to Taunton and Reading to Basingstoke lines to the 'slow' lines via an underpass below, rather than on the level; this removed a bottleneck that had plagued the route for decades. Five extra platforms were added under the plans, with the net result of at least four extra trains in each direction every hour. Paddington to Penzance trains were diverted to run from Waterloo in December 2010 while a new bridge was installed at Reading. Much of the planned electrification work on the Paddington-Bristol route was made far easier than upgrading any other route in Britain by the fact that Brunel built it for his Big Railway — broader tracks, and taller, wider locomotives and carriages.

Yet what about Brunel's rich legacy on the ground today?

In recent years there have been moves to have the entire Paddington to Bristol Temple Meads line designated as a UNESCO World Heritage Site, placing it on a similar footing to Stonehenge, the Taj Mahal and the Great Wall of China. Proponents consider it to be one of the finest examples of an early trunk railway anywhere in the world — despite the fact that its original gauge was changed — because so many of its original features have survived the passage of time.

Inevitably, the big question was asked: what is going to happen to the numerous historical structures big and small on the railway when it is adapted for electrification?

English Heritage, in conjunction with Network Rail, staged a wide-ranging public consultation exercise regarding the heritage features — not only on Brunel's GWR main line but also on adjacent routes which are part of the electrification project. In all, 100 bridges and tunnels face modification work or even demolition and replacement in order to accommodate the new overhead wires.

The exercise identified 35 structures, many of them, like the brick-built Silly Bridge in Oxfordshire and the Tudor Gothic stone Pixash Lane Bridge near Bath, being obscure in comparison to the classic features such as Maidenhead Bridge and Sonning Cutting, which were subsequently granted the protection of listed building status by the Department for Culture Media and Sport. In addition, other structures had their listings upgraded to give a stronger level of protection from future development.

The world-famous Box Tunnel in Wiltshire, one of the most extensive of the pioneering Great Western tunnels, and one of the most distinctive and best-loved landmarks on Brunel's Big Railway, was given Grade II listing, while Brunel's Sydney Gardens Footbridge in Bath was upgraded to Grade II*, the second highest grade for listed buildings.

Had electrification been available to Brunel, he would have certainly gone down that route. As it was, the only 'modern' traction system available to him was the somewhat curious atmospheric propulsion technology of the day which he tried out on the South Devon Railway and which spectacularly failed within a short time.

Yet just as Brunel wove neo-classical beauty into so many of his designs, big and small, we now have the great responsibility of conserving as much of his heritage as possible alongside a super-fast railway for the modern age and beyond.

In its new electrified incarnation, Brunel's original main line will again take its place at the forefront of domestic rail travel, and who knows, it may well hold more landmark surprises for the generations to come.

CHAPTER ONE

Bristol and its darkest days

P EOPLE HAVE lived in the Bristol area for at least 60,000 years, and the Romans had villas there, but it was only around 1000AD that the future city was founded, taking its name Brycgstow from the Old English words for 'the place at the bridge'.

Twenty years later, it had developed as a trading centre and even had its own mint — churning out silver pennies bearing the town's name. Its port developed in the 11th century at the point where the River Frome met the tidal River Avon, next to the original Bristol Bridge and just outside the fortified town walls.

In Norman times it boasted one of the strongest castles in southern England and by the 12th century it handled much of England's trade with Ireland. A new stone bridge was built in 1247 and the prosperous town expanded to absorb neighbouring villages to the point where, in 1373, Bristol became a county of its own, separate from Gloucestershire and Somerset.

As a natural extension of its activities as a mainstream trading port, Bristol next took off as a centre for shipbuilding and manufacturing, and by the 14th century it was one of the four biggest settlements in England, along with London, York and Norwich.

Its expansion was brought to an abrupt halt by the Black Death in 1348-1349, but by the 15th century Bristol was the second most important port in England, trading with Ireland, Gascony and Iceland. It was also the starting point of many key voyages of exploration, including expeditions across the Atlantic to find the mythological land of Hy-Brazil.

The Italian merchant, explorer and navigator Giovanni Caboto or John Cabot moved with his family to Bristol in 1490. It was a career move, as he could use the port as a launch pad for a voyage to the New World, following in the wake of the expeditions of Christopher Columbus.

Henry VII agreed to fund such a voyage, and on May 2, 1497, Cabot set sail on his ship the *Matthew*, a barque under 100 tons and crewed by 18 hands.

He reached land on June 9, either Cape Breton Island or Labrador, but thought he had found an island off the coast of China and did not realise it was a continent in its own right. He set off back to Bristol on June 26 and arrived in August to a hero's welcome. The king was so pleased that he gave him £10, equivalent to about two years' pay for an ordinary labourer or craftsman, and a pension of £20 a year.

Cabot took five ships to Newfoundland and Nova Scotia on February 3 the following year. There is controversy about the fate of the expedition: it has long been held that it was lost at sea, but more recent research suggests that Cabot had returned to Bristol by 1500. The date and manner of his death are not known but Cabot is held to have led the first European encounter with the mainland of North America since the Norse Vikings' visits to Vinland in the 11th century.

Bristol merchants followed in his footsteps to the New World. In 1499, William Weston headed the first English-led expedition to North America. There are some who have claimed that the name America derives not from the Italian explorer Amerigo Vespucci, who established that the land discovered by Columbus was not part of the east coast of Asia and instead constituted an entirely separate landmass, but from that of a Bristol-based Welshman, Richard Ameryk.

In 1910, Alfred E Hudd, a member of the Clifton Antiquarian Club, published a paper in which he pointed out that the senior Collector of

Customs of the Port of Bristol who probably handed over the money to Cabot was Ameryk. Hudd claimed that Cabot then named the 'new found land' in Ameryk's honour.

On his return from Newfoundland, Cabot had given one of the islands he had found to a friend and another to his barber. He also told a group of Italian friars that they could be bishops. If he was so liberal with favours, why not bestow one on the official who was handing him a personal fortune?

Hudd also mentions a lost manuscript of 1497 which referred to the discovery of America by Bristol merchants — several years before the name was well known on the continent. Whatever the origin of the name, Bristol became a major embarkation point for voyages to America, both of exploration and settlement, followed by trade.

In the 16th century, however, Bristol merchants focused far more on trade with Spain and its American colonies, even when such activities were banned during the Anglo-Spanish War of 1585-1604. Bristol's illicit trade soared in the second half of the 16th century and became a keystone of the local economy.

The transformation of the former Abbey of St Augustine into Bristol Cathedral in 1542 elevated the port to city status. By the 17th century, the days of Spain and Portugal as world powers were waning, and England's American colonies were gaining in importance for Bristol traders, especially during the Commonwealth of Oliver Cromwell, when trade with North America and the Caribbean flourished.

Bristol fishermen who had worked the Grand Banks of Newfoundland since the 15th century began settling in Newfoundland permanently in larger numbers in the 17th century, establishing colonies at Bristol's Hope and Cuper's Cove.

Bristol experienced rapid growth in the 18th century, when it was the second biggest port in England after London, mainly exporting woollen cloth, as well as coal, lead and animal skins, with regular trade routes to France, Ireland, Portugal, Spain and Africa's Barbary Coast. Imports included grain, slate, timber, wine and olive oil.

However, these were also the darkest decades, indeed centuries, of the city's history, when it played a pivotal part in the African slave trade.

BRISTOL AND THE SLAVE TRADE

Neither Britain nor Bristol started the transatlantic slave trade, but as with many other countries, reaped rich dividends from it. European voyages of exploration around Africa led to the establishment of trade routes and then territorial conquest. Among the commodities bartered for were slaves; not only were members of the indigenous population seized by merchant ships, but also tribal warfare resulted in the victors selling their captives to the highest bidder.

The first European nation to take part in the transatlantic slave trade was Portugal in the mid to late 15th century. In 1562, Captain John Hawkins made the first known English slaving voyage to Africa, during the reign of Elizabeth I.

African slaves provided a ready source of labour for the colonies being established in the New World, in an age where the concept of universal human rights was alien by today's standards. Up to 1698, the London-based Royal African Company, which had been set up by the Stuart monarchy with London merchants, held a monopoly on African trade.

The company was established once Charles II was crowned and was run by his brother, the Duke of York, the future James II. Its initial purpose was to tap into the gold fields of the Gambia River discovered by the royalist army leader Prince Rupert during the Cromwell era, but it quickly became involved in the slave trade. By the 1680s, the company was shipping around 5000 slaves each year, many branded with the letters DY after the Duke of York, or RAC, the company's initials.

With the overthrow of James II in 1689 and the Glorious Revolution which installed William of Orange on the throne, the company stood to lose its monopoly — a fact which did not go unnoticed by Bristol merchants, some of whom, such as city Tory MP and churchman Edward Colston, had already been profiting from the slave trade. Colston, hailed as a local hero and benefactor who endowed schools and almshouses in the city, made much of his fortune from slavery.

He had joined the Royal African Company in 1680 and three years later became a member of Bristol's Society of Merchant Venturers, which from 1694 vigorously campaigned for an end to the monopoly on the African trade.

With the ending of the monopoly in 1698, the doors were opened for everyone to get in on the slave trade, including the Merchant Venturers, which was founded as a guild in Bristol by the 13th century and by Cabot's time was all but running the port and town. Indeed, the Merchant Venturers had helped fund Cabot's 1497 voyage.

Edward VI granted had a royal charter in 1552 giving the Merchant Venturers a monopoly on sea trade, and it played a major role in the establishment of the aforementioned Newfoundland colonies. Its central role in the Bristol slave trade is understandably regarded by its members today as an indelible stain.

The first Bristol slave ship was *The Beginning*, owned by Stephen Barker, who bought enslaved Africans and took them to the Caribbean.

Conditions on the slave ships were appalling even on a good day: the cargo (the African captives were not regarded as human beings) was packed in like sardines, and on each voyage, on average half of the slaves died before the Caribbean was reached. Starvation, disease and brutality were rife. Historians have calculated that between 1697 and 1807, 2108 Bristol ships, each holding around 250 captives, took part in the 'Triangular Trade'.

From Bristol, manufactured goods were taken to West Africa and exchanged for Africans. A crossing of the Atlantic to the West Indies was then made with the slaves. The journey back to Bristol brought plantation goods such as sugar, tobacco, rum, rice and cotton, as well as a handful of slaves, who had to endure a second Atlantic crossing before being sold to the British aristocracy as house servants.

It is estimated that Bristol ships carried around 500,000 slaves (about 20% of all slaves carried in British ships) during this period, with lucrative profits meaning that investors could double their money, despite the mortality rate.

By 1732, half the number of English ships involved in the slave trade came out of Bristol, which had superseded London as Britain's main slave trading port. Six years later, that dubious crown was seized by Bristol's great rival, Liverpool.

The trade brought multiple benefits to Bristol, with the fitting out of slave ships and the provision of arms for those involved providing much work for ordinary people and profits for factory owners. By the mid-18th century, it was estimated that 60% of all Bristolians, including several Merchant Venturers, were directly or indirectly associated with the slave trade.

Bristol's share of the market declined after 1748, and by the time of abolition in 1807 the city's ships handled just 2% of Britain's slave trade. Accordingly, few Bristol merchants objected to abolition. In 1787, the Committee for the Abolition of the Slave Trade was formed by a group of evangelical English Protestants who had joined forces with Quakers to end what they saw as a blight upon humanity, and within two decades had built up much support in Parliament.

The following year, a Merchant Venturer, Joseph Harford, became chairman of the first provincial committee to promote the abolition of the slave trade. The Bristol society itself petitioned against abolition in the following year. The abolitionists were led by long-time anti-slave trade campaigner William Wilberforce.

After 20 years of campaigning, the Slave Trade Act was passed by a crushing 283 votes for to 16 against on March 25, 1807, abolishing the trade in the British Empire... but not slavery itself. It was only with the Slavery Abolition Act of 1833 that slavery became illegal throughout the British Empire.

The USA abolished its own Atlantic slave trade on March 2 the same year, but not internal slavery, which was to last until the end of the Civil War in 1865. Britain pressed for other countries to end their participation in the trade, and they responded within a few years — Sweden in 1813, France in 1814, The Netherlands in 1817 and Spain in 1820.

Shameful and unjustifiable as the slave trade was, there has been a widespread modern tendency to portray it purely as a white colonist/supremacist phenomenon. While there are undisputedly core elements to back up this view; by way of balance, the raids on the coasts of England and elsewhere in western Europe by Barbary pirates and corsairs from western Africa are often overlooked. Not only would the crews of ships be seized and sold into slavery in Africa, but also ordinary people living on the shores of places like south-west England in the 17th century would be taken by raiding parties.

Between 1606 and 1619, corsairs seized 466 British ships; and between 1677 and 1680, 160 British ships were captured by Algerians. Around 1600, it was estimated that there were around 35,000 European Christian slaves held on the Barbary Coast.

In no way do such facts excuse the later actions by Britain and other supposedly more enlightened European countries in the slave trade, but they serve to illustrate that slavery was as much a "might is right/can do, will" phenomenon as a racist one.

In 2007, 200 years after the abolition of the trade, the Merchant Venturers joined with the Lord Mayor of Bristol and other civic representatives in signing a statement regretting Bristol's role in the slave trade.

REVERSING THE PORT'S DECLINE

From around 1850, Liverpool's star as a port was in its ascendancy. During the era of the slave trade, around half of Bristol's shipping was concerned with the importation of tobacco, but the city's burgeoning Lancashire rival threatened to take even bigger slices of it away.

Bristol's trade with the continent suffered another major setback in the 1790s with the wars against post-revolutionary France. And the end to the slave trade in 1807 was another negative factor in the city's fortunes, albeit by then a small one. At the same time, the big manufacturing centres of the Midlands and the north of England were taking full advantage of the technological fruits of the Industrial Revolution — and stealing a march on former havens of prosperity like Bristol.

The Merchant Venturers was making every effort to ensure easy and safe access to its port in a bid to bolster its trade and well-being. It had long campaigned for the right to establish an effective lighthouse on the island of Flat Holm, one of two in the Bristol Channel that guard the main shipping lanes into the port via the Severn estuary and tidal River Avon. The first light on the island was a basic brazier mounted on a wooden frame on the higher eastern part of the island plateau, but the Merchant Venturers repeatedly complained that this was inadequate.

In 1733, the society's John Elbridge presented a petition to Trinity House, the national authority which controlled the rights to establish lighthouses, for one to be erected on the island because of the dangers in the Bristol Channel, but was refused permission. Two years later, William Crispe of Bristol informed Trinity House that he had leased the island for 99 years from the Earl of Bute and offered to build a lighthouse at his own expense but was also turned down.

Matters came to a head in 1736 when 60 soldiers drowned after their ship came to grief on the Wolves rocks nearby. Crispe presented a new scheme to the Merchant Venturers on March 17, 1737, and received backing for another bid to Trinity House. The Merchant Venturers insisted that Crispe should find at least £900 of the finance needed to build the tower, in return for a lease at £5 a year. This was agreed and the first light was lit on December 1, 1737.

In 1819, Trinity House reached agreement with principal lessee William Dickenson to take over the light and raised the height of the tower from 69ft to 89ft. Further improvements came in 1825.

Making shipping lanes safer was all well and good, but what about the facilities in the port itself that were becoming outdated?

The passage up the Avon Gorge, which had made the Bristol Channel safe from invaders during medieval times, was being increasingly seen as inadequate, partially because of silting and also because the size of vessels was increasing. The vast tidal range of the Bristol Channel turned what was a safe mooring at high tide into glistening mudflats at low water, with ships marooned on their sides and risking damage to their hulls. By contrast, rival Liverpool could offer deepwater berths at all states of the tide.

By the start of the 19th century, the limitations of Bristol's docks were threatening the livelihoods of many businesses, and in 1802 William Jessop, the great English civil engineer who built canals, harbours and some early railways, proposed the creation of a floating harbour.

By installing a dam and lock at Hotwells, Bristol's harbour would remain full of water at all states of the tide.

The Bristol Docks Company was formed with the active involvement of the Merchant Venturers and Bristol Corporation in 1803. This new company was instrumental in creating the Floating Harbour, which was approved by Parliament, with construction beginning in May 1804. The £530,000 project also included the construction of Cumberland Basin, Bathurst Basin, the New Cut, a large wide stretch of the harbour in Hotwells and various other locks, bridges and a weir.

Jessop built Cumberland Basin with two entrance locks from the tidal Avon and a junction lock between the basin and the Floating Harbour, thereby maintaining the level of water in the harbour despite ships coming and going from the river estuary.

The harbour was officially opened on May 1, 1809, two years after the slave trade was outlawed. Physically, it was innovative and a huge success. Commercially, it was a near flop because excessive harbour dues had to be charged in a bid to recoup the cost.

Furthermore, Liverpool had beaten Bristol in this respect too, by nearly a century. The first commercial wet dock was built in Liverpool in 1715. By the start of the 19th century, 40% of the world's trade was passing through Liverpool and the construction of major buildings within the city mirrored this wealth.

Liverpool was linked to its hinterland of Manchester by the Mersey and Irwell Navigation and the Bridgwater Canal, just as Bristol was connected to Bath and London by the Kennet & Avon Canal, both dating from the previous century. Liverpool traders felt that the waterway owners were making excessive profits from their custom, and so looked for a modern and cheap alternative.

History records that the answer was a railway — and after much debate on the issue, one that was hauled not by horses or cables, but by steam locomotives.

THE BIGGEST BRISTOL BRIDGE

To cut a long but very important story short, the Liverpool & Manchester Railway featuring George and Robert Stephenson's *Rocket* opened on September 15, 1830, and became the world's first inter-city passenger line. When the world's first trunk railway, the Grand Junction Railway, opened on July 4, 1837, linking the Liverpool & Manchester via Newton Junction to

Crewe, Wolverhampton and Birmingham, and thereafter via the London & Birmingham Railway to the capital, Liverpool had gained a massive advantage over all of its rivals. Bristol and its Merchant Venturers looked on in alarm.

What if Bristol, too, were connected to London by a steam railway? The heydays of Bristol's prosperity brought about by the slave trade had gone and the tobacco trade was now at risk too, but could a railway bring forth a new golden age? And who could build it?

Nobody knows for sure when the first permanent crossing of the Avon at Bristol was built, but it would certainly have had great strategic importance. As stated above, the first stone crossing, Bristol Bridge, dated from the 13th century. Like the London Bridge of old, it had houses built on either side, some eventually growing to five storeys high and overhanging the muddy waters. To help pay the rent of the premises, many had shop fronts, using their position to profit from passers-by.

The volume of traffic through the narrow roadway left between the shop fronts made the bridge a hazard to those passing over it, and a new bridge, appropriately designed by James Bridges, replaced it in 1768.

A riot broke out in 1793 because of the high tolls charged to bridge users. City fathers looked at the possibility of providing a second crossing, but Admiralty rules insisted that any crossing must be high enough to allow tall-masted warships to enter the harbour.

The cost of building a bridge downstream would be colossal, with giant embankments and viaducts required. The least expensive means would be to build one across the narrowest part of the Avon Gorge — so high above the water level that shipping would not be troubled one jot.

When Bristol wine merchant William Vick died in 1753, he left £1000 in his will for the purpose of building a bridge between Clifton Down on the north bank and Leigh Woods on the south. The idea was that when the interest on the sum had grown to £10,000, the bridge could be built. The Society of Merchant Venturers later stepped in and founded the Clifton Suspension Bridge Trust based on the legacy.

In 1793, William Bridges, another aptly named engineer, published plans for a stone arch with abutments containing factories which would pay for the upkeep of the bridge, but wars with France scuppered the project.

Vick's legacy was examined again in 1829, when the money had reached £8000. It was evident that fulfilling his request to build a stone bridge would cost many more times that amount, and therefore would probably never happen. However, rapid advancements in civil engineering by this time, including bridge design, led to a rethink. That year, the Merchant Venturers announced a competition with a prize of 100 guineas for the most viable bridge — attracting 22 entries.

The great engineer Thomas Telford was called in by the trustees to judge the final selection, but he threw them all out — insisting that the maximum possible span was 577ft. Asked to produce a design of his own, Telford drew up plans for a suspension bridge supported on tall Gothic towers. However, his design was considered too extravagant and too expensive.

Parliamentary approval was gained in May 1830 for a less-costly wrought iron suspension bridge over which tolls would be charged to recoup the cost. The Venturers then organised a second competition with new judges. This time the winner was a 24-year-old engineer who had been staying in Bristol during a period of recuperation.

His design was for a suspension bridge with 240ft-high trendy Egyptian-style chain support towers with sphinxes on top, just like the pyramids. His name was Isambard Kingdom Brunel — none other than the son of Marc Isambard Brunel, the French-born British engineer who was at that moment building a tunnel beneath the River Thames at Rotherhithe, the modern world's first tunnel beneath a waterway.

Young Isambard rejected the advice of his father when drawing up his design. Marc argued that the bridge should have a central support, as it was impossible to build a bridge of single span length.

In a foretaste of what was to come in the next three decades, and a career that would forever grip the imagination of the British public, Isambard maintained he could deliver the 'impossible' single span on his blueprint. Building work on his bridge began amid civic celebrations on June 21, 1831.

However, the Bristol riots against the rejection of the second Reform Bill, which aimed to eradicate rotten boroughs and give cities such as

Bristol parliamentary representation, brought the works to a halt. Brunel was sworn in as a special constable as up to 600 men rioted.

The disorder saw a negative impact on investments in the city and subscriptions to the bridge company dried up, bringing a permanent halt to the works. Shortly after the launch ceremony, the bridge committee told Brunel that they did not yet have enough funds to complete it.

Isambard would not live to see his magnificent bridge completed. Yet his design had so impressed the Merchant Venturers, who by then had moved far away from the era of the city's slave trade, that the society appointed him to a far greater project, one that would leave him immortalised both in legend and history: the Great Western Railway.

CHAPTER TWO

Only the best will do

WITH LIVERPOOL'S star in the ascendancy, Bristol saw only too clearly the need for a state-of-the-art transport link to London, before it lost its dominance of the American trade for good.

Bristol had enjoyed excellent transport links with London for two centuries; firstly in the form of the Great West Road, and latterly with the construction of the Kennet & Avon Canal. Sections of the former had existed in parts before Roman times, but these became one unified route in 1635 as one of six 'great roads' built on the orders of King Charles I to facilitate postal deliveries.

A post office had been established in Bristol by the 1670s and letters from London took about three days to arrive. With the rise in popularity of Bath as a spa resort from the time of Queen Anne in the early 18th century, the road became known as the Bath Road.

As Bath's wealth blossomed and the rich and well-to-do patronised it as an early holiday resort, the road became improved by turnpike trusts which had the power to charge tolls. The first turnpike on the Great West Road was established between Reading and Theale in 1714. It was followed by sections between Kensington and Twyford three years later.

Many wealthy landowners co-operated with the turnpike trusts along the Great West Road, seeing money to be made, and its coaching towns and their inns, especially the midway point of Hungerford, prospered greatly during the stagecoach era.

In 1752, it took about two days to travel from London to Bristol. The improvement in road surfaces brought about by the turnpikes reduced that to 38 hours by 1782, and to 18 hours by 1836, when Royal Mail coaches could do it in less than 13 hours.

In 1830, six stagecoaches a day plied their trade between London and Bristol, and the figure had risen to 10 by 1836, with five separate coach operators in business.

Steam traction made its debut on the Great West Road, long before a steam railway locomotive plied its trade between London and Bristol.

Cornish inventor Goldsworthy Gurney designed and built several steam-powered road vehicles in the late 1820s, and in July 1829, one ran between London and Bath and back, averaging a speed of 14mph on the return journey.

This journey took place two months before the Rainhill Trials in which George and Robert Stephenson's *Rocket* paved the way for the future development of the railway steam locomotive as well as deciding on the form of traction to be used on the new Liverpool & Manchester Railway.

Was the world ready for such innovations? Not entirely, it appears. When Gurney's steam carriage passed through Melksham, it was attacked by townsfolk, and the stoker was injured. It had to be escorted under guard to Bath to prevent further attacks.

The carriage featured a water tube boiler, fired by coke, placed in the rear boot of the carriage. Steam was delivered to the two driving cylinders placed under the body. The carriage could carry six passengers inside and 12 outside.

THE KENNET & AVON CANAL

Britain's canal network facilitated much of the Industrial Revolution, providing a cheap and effective way of carrying bulk raw materials and manufactured products between ports, markets and factories.

It has always been possible to travel from London to Bristol by boat, but the passage of the English Channel, especially around Land's End, and Atlantic storms made such voyages hazardous, while shipping was often at risk from French privateers during times of conflict.

It was mooted as long ago as Elizabethan times that it might be possible to build a waterway linking Bristol, Bath and London, connecting the Bristol Avon to the Thames. In 1626, mathematician Henry Briggs surveyed both levels and saw that the land between them was easy to dig. Indeed, the headwaters of both rivers are only three miles apart at the narrowest point. Briggs proposed digging a canal between the two, but the plan died with him in 1630.

In the late 17th century, four parliamentary bills for such a waterway were defeated due to opposition from landowners who feared that revenue from turnpike roads would be lost. The River Kennet through Reading was made navigable in 1723 and the Bristol Avon from Bristol to Bath followed suit in December 1727, but these were primarily little local concerns.

A waterway linking the two, the Western Canal, was proposed in 1788 to serve Hungerford, Marlborough, Calne, Chippenham and Melksham. The name was soon changed to the Kennet & Avon Canal.

Following an initial survey in 1789, engineer John Rennie carried out a fresh survey in 1793, changing the course of the proposed canal to take in Great Bedwyn, Devizes, Trowbridge and Newbury. The Kennet & Avon Canal Act received Royal Assent on April 17, 1794, and building began. The Newbury to Hungerford section was completed in 1798, and the canal opened throughout in 1810.

Its major engineering features include the Dundas and Avoncliff aqueducts, Bruce Tunnel under Savernake Forest, pumping stations at Claverton and Crofton, and finally, the spectacular flight of Caen Hill Locks at Devizes.

The canal easily undercut road hauliers; the rate of carriage per ton from London to Bath was £2 9s 6d in 1810, compared to £6 3s 0d to £7 per ton by road.

The Kennet & Avon Canal Company bought the Kennet Navigation in 1812 for £100,000. This stretched from Newbury to the junction with the Thames at Kennet Mouth, near Reading, and four years later the company acquired a majority shareholding in the Avon Navigation.

The journey from Bath to Newbury took an average of three-and-a-half days. Much of the traffic was generated by the carriage of coal and Mendip stone via the feeder Somerset Coal Canal. By 1832, 300,000 tons of freight were carried annually.

These were impressive figures by the standards of the day, but paled in comparison when the potential of the Liverpool & Manchester Railway became clear. The Society of Merchant Venturers knew that they had to respond if Bristol's economy was to survive, and waterways by now were clearly not the answer.

COMETH THE HOUR…

The son of Marc Isambard Brunel and Sophia Kingdom Brunel, Isambard Kingdom Brunel, was born on April 9, 1806, in Portsmouth.

Young Isambard was not only to follow in his father's footsteps as one of the greatest engineers of his day, but with his big railway from London to Bristol, and the seaward 'extension' by which steamships would continue the journey onward to New York, would soon eclipse his fame.

The son of a wealthy farmer, Marc Brunel was born on April 25, 1769, in Hacqueville in northern France, and displayed a talent for drawing, mathematics and mechanics at a very early age — to the disdain of his father who wanted him to become a priest.

Marc enlisted as a cadet on a French naval frigate, but on returning home in 1792 became appalled by the revolutionary excesses of the Jacobins. He fled to England to escape the vengeance of a revolutionary mob, and met Sophia, then 17, the youngest of 16 children of Portsmouth naval contractor William Kingdom.

Marc Brunel subsequently made a fortune in the US, building the Bowery Theatre, an arsenal and a cannon foundry along with many other buildings in New York. He returned to England in 1799 and married Sophia in the parish church of St Andrew in Holborn on November 1 that year.

His business took off big time when the British government adopted his scheme for mechanising the manufacture of pulley-blocks for ships, which until then had been made by hand. Marc was given a £17,000 contract, and the Brunels moved from their home in London to Portsea near Portsmouth so he could take charge of the project.

He went on to design huge steam-powered machines for sawing and bending timber, as well as machines for stocking knitting, printing and the mass production of boots and shoes. His achievements were publicly recognised in 1814 when he was elected to the Royal Society.

Marc also installed a log handling and sawmill at the naval dockyard in Chatham. Buying, storing and handling timber was a major problem and expense for the navy at the time, as a typical battleship needed 2000 mature oak trees, with much of the timber being imported from Russia. Once on site, the wood had to be seasoned and stored.

Few saw any significance in what was a minor detail at the time, but the sawmill was served by a railway with rails placed 7ft apart.

While he was working at Chatham, Marc observed the marine ship-worm *teredo navalis* in action, boring through the toughest timbers. This worm was a curse on seafarers throughout the world, and was said to have sunk more ships than any enemy action.

The boring action of the shipworm, however, gave Brunel the inspiration for a method of tunnelling through soft ground, and possibly beneath a river. However, despite his resourcefulness in the world of technology, he paid scant attention to his financial affairs.

His bankers west bust in 1820 and in May 1821, Marc and Sophia were incarcerated in the King's Bench debtors' prison for three months — until the Duke of Wellington persuaded the government to pay £5000 to prevent his services being lost to Russia, where the tsar was keen on him building a river bridge.

Isambard attended boarding school in Hove, Sussex, and carried out a survey of the town while he was there. At 14, he was sent to the College of Caen in Normandy, and progressed from there to the Lycee Henri-Quatre in Paris. Marc arranged for him to have an apprenticeship under world-famous clockmaker Abraham Louis Breguet. Returning to England in August 1822, after his father's financial troubles had subsided, Isambard set to work in his father's office on yet more inventions, including two suspension bridges for the French government and the world's first double-acting marine engine.

The father-and-son team laid claim to their place in history with the building of the Thames Tunnel, hailed in its day as the eighth wonder of the world. The growth of the port London in the wake of the opening of the first enclosed docks on the Isle of Dogs in 1802 led to warehouses mushrooming on both sides of the river, but there was no means of communicating between them other than by boat.

Clearly a physical crossing downstream of London Bridge was needed but with the technology of the day it was not possible to build one high enough to allow ships to pass below.

Ancient stories held that the Assyrian queen Semiramis had a tunnel built beneath the River Euphrates at Babylon, and therefore a tunnel was a possibility. Mine workings in west Cornwall by then had extended beneath the seabed, so the legend was becoming but a scientific possibility.

In 1802, Robert Vazie and Richard Trevithick announced plans for a shorter tunnel on the comparatively narrow section of the river between Rotherhithe and Limehouse, the boring of a 5ft-high pilot tunnel on the south bank starting in August 1807. They reached the low tide mark on the north shore six months later, but the project was abandoned with only 200ft to go due to problems caused by quicksand and frequent flooding.

In stepped Marc Brunel, who in 1818 patented a tunnelling shield which made safe excavations through water-bearing strata possible. The construction of a tunnel under the Thames was advocated by the Duke of Wellington and the Thames Tunnel Company was formed in 1824, with Brunel senior as engineer. The first shaft was sunk at Rotherhithe on March 2, 1825, and Isambard was brought in as acting resident engineer 13 months into the proceedings.

The poisonous waters of the Thames, laden with sewage bacteria as at that stage the capital had no proper waste disposal system, broke into the tunnel workings on five occasions.

Isambard was so enthusiastic about the ground-breaking project that he regularly remained in the tunnel for 36 hours at a time to supervise the work. He was inside on January 12, 1828, when floodwaters burst into the tunnel again. He ran for the exit with two other men but the floodwaters knocked him down. He was swept unconscious to a locked emergency exit, which a fellow engineer then opened just in time to rescue him.

Six workmen died in the flood, including the two who had been standing beside Brunel when the breach occurred. The accident led to the tunnel works going on hold for several years (it was finally opened on March 25, 1843, the day after Marc Brunel was knighted by Queen Victoria), and although he had lived to tell the tale, Isambard was severely injured.

He spent several months convalescing in Brighton, but his doctors were concerned that he was not recovering as quickly as he should have been. Sources blamed this fact on 'exertions with actresses', and so it was decided to send him to a more sedate and refined location where such distractions would not be as readily available.

Clifton, the genteel western suburb of Bristol, was chosen. One of the oldest and most affluent areas of the city, with many fine Georgian houses, much of it was constructed with profits from tobacco and the slave trade.

In 1676, the Merchant Venturers acquired the Manor of Clifton including 220 acres of Clifton Down bordering the Avon Gorge. Two centuries later, the neighbouring Manor of Henbury, which included Durdham Down, came on the market. The Venturers agreed with the Corporation of Bristol that if the latter bought this land, the pair would join forces to dedicate 440 acres for the use and enjoyment of the citizens of Bristol in perpetuity.

Clifton Down and Durdham Down are a much-loved beauty spot next to the suspension bridge. Under the provisions of the Clifton and Durdham Downs Act 1861, the Downs are still administered by a Downs Committee appointed in equal numbers by the city council and the Venturers. Clifton itself was formally incorporated into the city in the 1830s.

It was at Clifton in 1829 that Isambard entered a competition to build a bridge to span the gorge, as described in the last chapter. His contributions to the Thames Tunnel and his plans for the Clifton bridge — both of which were then far from complete — earned him election as a Fellow of the Royal Society on June 10, 1830, at the age of 24.

However, he still had to earn a living wage. To this end, he arranged and oversaw the drainage of marshland at Tollesbury in Essex and then designed Monkwearmouth's North Dock, on which work began in 1838. As far as railways were concerned, eager to see what all the international fuss was about, on December 5, 1831, he had taken a trip on the Liverpool & Manchester Railway, but unlike most other passengers, remained unimpressed. He knew he could do better.

In his notebook, he wrote: "I record this specimen of the shaking on Manchester railway. The time is not far off when we shall be able to take our coffee and write while going noiselessly and smoothly at 45mph — let me try."

He also visited the Stockton & Darlington Railway, which had opened in 1825 as the world's first steam-hauled public line.

Nicholas Roch, who had been enlisted alongside Isambard as a special constable during the aforementioned Reform Bill riots, sat on the Committee for Bristol Docks. The Reform Act, which enlarged the vote and was welcomed by city dwellers, was passed in 1832, leading to a renewed confidence in both Bristol and the national economy.

Funding became available to improve the Floating Harbour and Roch recommended the appointment of Isambard, who advised on the installation of sluices and an underfall dam for regulating water inflow and scouring silt.

BRISTOL'S FIRST RAILWAY SCHEMES

The railway concept had been around since the time of ancient Greece and formed the backbone of the Industrial Revolution, with horse and man-worked tramways laid both underground in mines and on the surface to carry coal and extracted ore to the nearest transhipment point — usually a navigable waterway or harbour.

These pre-steam era early railways, tramways and plateways were laid purely to serve local concerns. One such line was the 10-mile Bristol & Gloucestershire Railway which, opened throughout in 1835, linked collieries near Coalpit Heath with the River Avon at Bristol using horse traction.

However, with the invention of the steam railway locomotive by Richard Trevithick and its first public demonstration in 1804, thoughts of a few visionaries turned towards the idea of a national network of railways.

English lawyer, surveyor, land agent and pioneer rail promoter William James, a man grossly overlooked by history in favour of contemporaries such as the Stephensons, originally came up with the idea of a railway linking Liverpool and Manchester in 1822.

He surveyed other lines at a time when the idea of cross-country railways was generally considered absurd. During the Napoleonic Wars in 1815, he wrote to the Prince Regent proposing a rail link between the two principal naval dockyards at Chatham and Portsmouth which in peacetime could be used for passenger traffic.

In 1820, he promoted a horse-worked Central Junction Railway from Stratford-upon-Avon to Paddington, linking to the Stratford-upon-Avon Canal at Bancroft Basin which would carry goods and raw materials to and from Birmingham and the Black Country. Only part of the line was ever built, the Stratford & Moreton Tramway.

Plans for a horse-worked line along the main road from Bristol to London had been drawn up as early as 1800 by Dr John Anderson, but nothing came of his proposals at that time. Fresh plans were published by the London and Bristol Railroad Company in December 1824 and the route was surveyed by John Loudon McAdam, the famous road engineer whose name was adopted for road surfacing material. It ran through Mangotsfield, Marshfield, Wootton Bassett and the Vale of White Horse to Wantage and Wallingford, and from there to London, either via Reading or an alternative route on the south bank of the Thames. McAdam chose the flattest route possible.

Even this stalled due to lack of interest and consequent lack of finance, however, as did a plan by Francis Fortunes for a General Junction Railroad from London to Bristol, and a London to Reading scheme backed by Kennet & Avon Canal shareholders the following year.

The situation changed with the opening and meteoric rise of the Liverpool & Manchester Railway. At the same time, it was noted that the canal link between Bristol and London was not always reliable: low water levels could strand boats in hot weather, and in winter, frost and floods hampered traffic. When boats could not pass, goods had to be transferred to road at huge cost.

Proposals for a Bristol & London Railway, quickly changed to London & Bristol Railway, appeared in May 1832, with a direct but hilly route via Bath, Bradford-on-Avon, Trowbridge, Devizes, Hungerford, Newbury and Reading. The survey was undertaken by William Brunton and Henry Price. Yet again, the necessary finance was not made available.

However, that autumn four Bristol businessmen, George Jones and William Harford, who were directors of the Bristol & Gloucestershire Railway, sugar refiner Thomas Guppy (a close friend of Isambard) and chemist William Tothill, met at an office in Temple Becks and formed a railway committee. They then proceeded to muster up sufficient support among city merchants and financiers.

A meeting was held on January 21, 1833, between the Merchant Venturers, who had supported Isambard over the suspension bridge project, Bristol Corporation, the Bristol Dock Company, the Chamber of Commerce and the Bristol & Gloucestershire Rail Road Company to look at such a scheme.

Agreement was reached to fund a survey of the route and Roch was asked to find an engineer. That was not an easy task during the formative days of railways, when individuals with experience of such works were very thin on the ground.

Roch alerted his friend Isambard to the project, and he and several rivals including Brunton and Price, along with William Townsend, who had built the Bristol & Gloucestershire Railway, were invited to find the cheapest route.

Brazenly, Isambard, still only 27 years of age, told the railway committee that despite the false starts of the third part of a century, he would not build a railway on the cheap. He said he would either be given the scope to build the best railway of them all, or was not interested.

He called their bluff, and won the day... but only by a single vote.

Isambard Kingdom Brunel was appointed as engineer to what soon became known as the Great Western Railway — a major milestone in global transport history.

CHAPTER THREE

The broad blueprint takes shape

B RISTOL'S RAILWAY committee ordered Isambard to survey the
route for his railway within a month. And so, on March 9, 1833, he
and William Townsend, who had agreed to become his subordi-
nate, set out on horseback to survey a route from Bristol to Bath.

However, Townsend quickly found that he could not keep up with the
younger man's horse riding and agreed to remain behind in Bristol to
work under his instructions.

Isambard was now on his own, a position he relished. His big chance
had come and he was determined to let his imagination run riot — to show
the world how everything could be so much better.

He looked at two alternative routes, one via Bradford, Devizes,
Marlborough, Newbury and Reading, and the other crossing hilly terrain
to Chippenham and then running through a comparatively sparsely popu-
lated area to Reading.

He rode up to 40 miles each day, and on one occasion his horse fell on
the way home.

His scheme, estimated to cost £2.8 million, was formally launched
at Bristol Guildhall on July 30, 1833, when it was decided to set up a
company to build the line, including directors from both Bristol and

London. The 116-mile line itself would cost £2.5 million.

Up to this point there had been separate Bristol and London committees but now the first joint meeting of the London & Bristol Railroad was held at the offices of Gibbs & Sons in Lime Street, London, on August 22, 1833. Five days later, Isambard's appointment as engineer of the line was confirmed.

The name Great Western Railway appeared for the first time when the company prospectus was issued shortly afterwards. Isambard hired an office at 53 Parliament Street in London and appointed a draughtsman and a chief clerk.

Before any proper surveying could take place, however, Isambard had to bring the landowners on side. Many of them started out from a position of outrage, so it was up to Isambard to use his diplomatic skills to the utmost. In the case of Berkshire MP Robert Palmer, Isambard agreed to build a mile-long tunnel through Sonning Hill so that the railway could not be seen from his house.

Not only did Brunel want access to their land, he also needed their word that they would not oppose the company's Bill when it came before parliament. He also had to persuade investors to come up with the necessary finance. It was a Herculean undertaking.

Nine months after he had left Bristol on horseback for that first survey, plans for his railway were lodged in the Parliamentary Bills Office and there was fierce opposition from the outset. The canal and stagecoach companies were understandably (and in both cases, justifiably) against the railway, and farmers near London were worried about cheaper produce coming from further afield.

Even the provost of Eton College expressed concern — because the railway would make it easier for its upper-crust pupils to access the brothels of London.

The Great Western Railway Bill was passed in the House of Commons by 182 votes to 92 in March 1834, but it then had to go before a committee.

This committee, chaired by Lord Granville Somerset, met on April 16 — and then sat for 57 days to discuss the bill! More objectors appeared, some claiming that passengers would be "smothered in tunnels" and "necks would be broken," while a farmer expressed concern that his cattle would die if they passed beneath a railway bridge.

The Bill was eventually approved by the committee but was then rejected by the House of Lords on July 25, 1834, by 47 votes to 30. One of the principal objections came from residents of Brompton who did not want the London terminus to be sited at Vauxhall. Opposition also came from the promoters of the London & Southampton Railway – who proposed making a branch from their line to serve Bath and Bristol. However, by then public support had grown to the point whereby parliament's final approval was all but assured.

The railway company issued a new prospectus in September 1834 for a railway running via Bath, Chippenham, Wootton Bassett, Swindon, Wantage, Reading, Maidenhead and Slough, and with a terminus at Euston where the railway would join the London & Birmingham.

Although not as direct as the earlier route taking in Bradford, Hungerford and Devizes, it offered access to big towns further afield, such as Oxford and Cheltenham, via branch lines. It would therefore tap into the lucrative Gloucestershire wool trade, with the South Wales coalfield a prize goal on the horizon beyond the River Severn. A longer route, yes, but a far more strategic one: instead of serving small market towns, it would link Bristol and London to big centres of population and industry.

Meanwhile, the offer to build the mile-long Sonning Tunnel had failed to mollify Palmer, so Brunel reduced its length by 625 yards to make it cheaper.

The Great Western Railway Bill received royal assent from King William IV on August 31, 1835. The Act incorporated the Great Western Railway Company and authorised it to raise £2.5 million for building a line from London to Bristol through the parishes of Box, Ditteridge, Corsham, Lacock, Chippenham, Hardenhuish, Langley Burrell, Kington St Michael, Draycot Cerne, Sutton Benger, Christian Malford, Bremhill, Foxham, Dauntsey, Brinkworth, Wootton Bassett, Wroughton, Lydiard Tregoze, Swindon, Stratton St Margaret, Stanton Fitzwarren, Highworth, and South Marston. Branches were authorised from Thingley to a point near the gasworks in Trowbridge and from Holt to Kingston Farm near Bradford. Building work started within a month.

THE 'BIG BIG RAILWAY'

Isambard set out to build the best railway possible, and by its very nature, it would also be the biggest. He wanted a luxury people carrier which would be the pride of all Britain.

He had been unimpressed by the Liverpool & Manchester, which had been built to George Stephenson's gauge of 4ft 8½in.

This choice was based on Stephenson's measurements of the space between the wheels of coal carts in north-east England. Freight would be the main source of traffic on railways in that region, and as common carriers, railways had to be capable of accepting private owners' horse-drawn wagons. Accordingly, the Stockton & Darlington Railway was originally designed to a 4ft 8in gauge, with an additional half-inch later added to reduce friction. This 4ft 8½in gauge subsequently became known in Britain and then much further afield as standard gauge.

Brunel showed his disdain for the often uncomfortable motion of the four-wheel carriages on the Liverpool & Manchester. His railway would be transporting the well-to-do to places like Bath, and he wanted accommodation that would suit them accordingly. So he ripped up the Stephenson rule book and sought a wider gauge, which would allow bigger rolling stock and locomotives with wheels placed outside their frames — allowing for bigger boilers and greater capacity for speed. The lower centre of gravity would allow trains to run more steadily and safely.

He wanted to reduce the rolling resistance of carriage and wagon stock. A wider gauge would allow larger wheel diameters, lessening the effect of friction while facilitating the ability to build wide carriages with bodies mounted as low as possible, minimising air resistance. In short, the bigger they are, the more they will carry and the faster they will go.

In the defeated Great Western Railway Bill of 1834, the gauge had been restricted to standard. By the time the next Bill was lodged, Isambard wanted a gauge of 7ft and so asked Lord Shaftesbury, who was drafting the Bill, to leave out the gauge limitation. When questioned by a member of Shaftesbury's staff about the problem of the break of gauge, and the fact that his trains would not be interchangeable with standard gauge lines, Isambard said he did not consider the problem to be significant.

He was therefore aware of the issue and knew that building broad gauge would be more expensive because of the larger tunnels, cuttings and embankments that would be needed; but did he foresee the extent to which the problem would literally divide the country for the rest of that century?

By and large, Brunel took the view that his railway would serve only the region through which it was built and did not need to take account of the gauge of other railways.

When debating the Bill, and hearing all sorts of absurd objections to steam railways, MPs failed to pick up on the omission of a gauge clause. And so, purely by chance, the door was left open for Isambard to choose any gauge he liked.

On September 15, 1835, he proposed a broad gauge of between 6ft 10in and 7ft to the GWR board, producing mathematical and scientific reasons as to why it was superior to Stephenson's system, rather than developing 4ft 8½in gauge to suit his needs.

On October 29, 1835, the GWR board approved Brunel's proposal for a broad gauge. The chosen 7ft gauge, publicly announced at the company's half-yearly meeting in Bristol in August 1836, was identical to that of the Chatham sawmill rope-worked railway that his father Marc had laid. The extra quarter inch that made it 7ft 0¼in gauge was added to give slack to locomotives built to this very much wider than normal specification.

One problem that did worry Brunel about the broad gauge was the proposed junction with the London & Birmingham north of Euston. However, that issue was solved when the GWR fell out with the London & Birmingham and looked for a new London terminus site instead.

That site was found adjoining the canal basin in Paddington where, initially, a temporary station was built (see Chapter 4) — eventually catapulting what had been a small village to the west of the capital to world transport prominence.

Brunel's broad gauge trackwork not only differed from methods used in the rest of the country in terms of the spacing of its rails; while the Stephensons laid their tracks on closely spaced stone blocks, later superseded by sleepers, Brunel considered that cross timbers would be too expensive for broad gauge.

As ever, he consequently came up with his own unique solution.

He designed a special rail section known as bridge rail. This rail was supported along its entire length on longitudinal timbers which were joined at intervals by cross timbers. By employing this method, Brunel calculated that a light rail section of only 43lb per yard was necessary.

The flaw here was that the ballast, which was packed beneath the timbers, settled, leaving the track supported only by the piles which had been driven into the ground to hold the longitudinal timbers, making riding uncomfortable in places, something Brunel had certainly not planned.

It was not only Brunel and his GWR that chose to differ from 4ft 8½in gauge. The Eastern Counties Railway, for instance, chose 5ft gauge, but soon realised that lack of compatibility was a mistake and converted to Stephenson gauge. There were also several early lines in Scotland built to 5ft 6in gauge, but soon changed to standard gauge. The first railway in Ireland, the Dublin and Kingstown, was built to 4ft 8½in, but the Ulster Railway, on the advice of the Irish Railway Commission, used 6ft 2in.

The Dublin & Drogheda Railway began building its new line to 5ft 2in to cut costs, and the Board of Trade in 1843 recommended the use of 5ft 3in, the norm on both sides of the Irish border today. This unusual track gauge is otherwise found only in parts of Australia and in Brazil.

CHAPTER FOUR

The Great Western adventure begins

BUILDING WORK began within four weeks of the Great Western Railway Bill receiving royal assent. The first contract for building part of the Great Western Railway was let in September 1835.

On the first section of the line, Isambard had designed an 891ft long viaduct across the River Brent at Hanwell to the west of London. It comprised eight demi-elliptical brick arches with a span of 70ft, the highest being 65ft, and was named after Lord Wharncliffe, who had helped the Great Western Railway Bill through the House of Lords. It carries his coat of arms to this day.

It was to be the first of many stupendous structures designed by Brunel and built under his auspices. The contractor was the partnership of Thomas Grissell and Samuel Morton Peto and the cost was £40,000. Just as with his initial design for the Clifton Suspension Bridge, Isambard chose an Egyptian design for Wharncliffe Viaduct, following the contemporary trend of neo-classical architecture.

When building began in 1836, a large group of Irish navvies working on the railway went to the Stag pub where a dispute broke out with some

Englishmen. The Irishmen then turned their rage on a local magistrate who had called the police. Three of them were subsequently jailed for two months, with magistrates warning the GWR in a letter that unless order was maintained during the viaduct's construction, it might be necessary to apply to the Government for a body of police or soldiers to be stationed at Hanwell.

The first locomotives to cross the viaduct were *Vulcan* and the *Aeolus* built by Tayleur & Co of Warrington and *North Star*, built by Robert Stephenson & Co at Newcastle-upon-Tyne. It is said locally that Queen Victoria enjoyed the view from the viaduct over the Brent valley so much that she often asked the Royal Train to stop there.

The viaduct was also the first on a railway to have a commercial electrical telegraph system. Brunel saw the advantages of the pioneer electric telegraph system for use in running a railway and in 1838 he persuaded Sir Charles Wheatstone and William Fothergill Cooke to install their five-needle telegraph system between Paddington and West Drayton. Experiments proved successful and the telegraph came into use on April 9, 1839.

On New Year's Day 1845, killer John Tawell was arrested following the use of a needle telegraph message from Slough to Paddington. He is believed to be the first person to be arrested as the result of telecommunications technology, and it is thought to be the first known homicide case where the criminal attempted to flee by train.

The message was: "A murder has just been committed at Salt Hill and the suspected murderer was seen to take a first class ticket to London by the train that left Slough at 7.42pm. He is in the garb of a Quaker with a brown greatcoat on which reaches his feet. He is in the last compartment of the second first-class carriage."

Tawell was convicted of the murder of his mistress, Sarah Hart, by administering prussic acid, and was hanged in public on March 28, 1845, at Aylesbury with huge crowds watching. The telegraph transmitter and receiver used to apprehend Tawell are preserved in the Science Museum in London.

As built, the viaduct carried two broad gauge tracks, but was widened in 1890, the extra north pier matching Isambard's original two, and today the structure carries four. It is considered to be of such historical importance that in 1949 it became one of the first structures anywhere to be given listed building protection.

THE FIRST TRAINS RUN

Isambard Kingdom Brunel married Mary Horsley in Kensington church on July 5, 1836, after which the couple went on honeymoon to North Wales and the West Country. She was the brother of painter John Horsley, a member of the Royal Academy, who later painted Brunel's portrait.

Even during his honeymoon in Cheltenham, Brunel never lost sight of the task in hand. GWR company secretary Charles Alexander Saunders met him midway through to brief him on how the line was progressing. The couple moved into a fashionable residential home at 18 Duke Street, between Piccadilly and Pall Mall. The site is now occupied by the Colonial Office.

By this time, his financial worries were all but over. He could easily afford his luxury home on his £2000-a-year salary from the GWR, and could sustain a family. Isambard and Mary had three children, including Henry Marc, who became an engineer in his own right and worked on Tower Bridge with railway engineer Beauchamp Tower, inventor of the spherical engine. Completing a unique circle, Henry Marc crossed the Thames in the air, while his father and grandfather had burrowed beneath it.

Having earlier considered a terminus at Euston and then Vauxhall, Brunel eventually chose Paddington, on the outskirts of the city of London. The first station to open there was a basic temporary terminus on the west side of Bishop's Bridge Road; not the GWR's finest moment by any means, nor did it pretend to be. It opened on June 4, 1838, along with the first GWR service, covering the 22½ miles from London to 'Maidenhead' (also referred to as Maidenhead Riverside) station at Taplow. After the opening of the permanent station on May 29, 1854, it became the site of the goods depot.

The London to 'Maidenhead' section opened to paying passengers on Whit Monday, June 4, 1838, although a directors' special had been run five days before, hauled by *North Star*. This VIP special made the inaugural run from Paddington to Maidenhead at 11am on May 31. Paddington station was decorated, and when the signal was given at 11am sharp, the six-coach train steamed out amid the cheers of a large crowd of spectators.

This first train was made up of several classes of coach. There was an 'extra first' saloon with large plate-glass windows, sofas, cushions, and tables. The 'ordinary' first class coaches had three compartments, each accommodating eight passengers, and equipped with sunblinds. The second class coaches were closed, but the third class were open to the air.

The passengers were the GWR directors, a large party of MPs and other dignitaries. Looking out of the windows, the passengers glimpsed Kensal Green, Wormwood Scrubs and the "picturesque little village of Acton" before arriving at Ealing, which was decorated with flags and banners.

A passenger later wrote: "The route taken was then by Hanwell, Southall, and Drayton, through a beautifully wooded and fertile district, and the sudden transition from the smoke, dust, and noise of London to the quiet glades and shady thickets of the park-like country we were then traversing, appeared more like the work of magic than the result of the ingenuity and labour of man." If only those areas were like that today!

Maidenhead was reached 49 minutes after the train had left Paddington, giving an average speed of 28mph. The driver had been instructed to proceed with caution because construction work was still in progress at several places on the route. Maidenhead was seen as an ideal first temporary terminus for the GWR. It lay on the Bath road, part of the Great West Road, and was the main exit from London to the west.

The GWR had compiled data which showed that on average, 70 coaches a day passed through Maidenhead — more than any other town in Britain. So the first station serving the town was built on the Bath road, adjoining Dumb Bell Bridge, which takes the railway over the public highway.

One early source of revenue for the new railway was the carriage of road coaches on trucks from Maidenhead to Paddington, a foretaste of the Motorail services run by British Rail in the Sixties. The road coaches were therefore able to cut their journey time by two thirds. One of the more prominent Bath stagecoaches, the Beaufort Hunt coach, took advantage of this facility almost from the opening of the line. Soon, however, stage-coaches themselves would be no more, thanks to the success of railways.

After the passengers on the VIP train inspected the works and building at the Maidenhead terminus, the train returned to Salt Hill, near Slough, where a "substantial repast" was served in a large marquee erected for the occasion. At this function, Edward Divett, the MP for Exeter, made a speech in which he mentioned the possibility of booking a journey from London to New York. This point was emphasised because a few days previously, as we shall see, Brunel's first paddle-wheel steamship the SS *Great Western* had completed its maiden voyage to New York and back.

Another MP, a Mr Guest (presumably Josiah John Guest, the first MP for Merthyr Tydfil), toasted the health of Brunel "to whose exertions and skill we are so much indebted". Brunel, he said, had "stepped out of the ordinary track" and he believed no other man would have had the courage to do so.

The public opening day began with an 8am departure from Paddington behind *North Star,* with around 200 passengers on board. The train attained a speed of 36mph.

The Windsor and Eton Express reported the proceedings as follows: "On Monday, this stupendous undertaking was opened to the public from the terminus at Paddington to the station at Maidenhead, and the ease with which the various journeys were conducted, added to the rapidity of the trains, was such as at once to inspire the public with confidence in the safety of the engines, and the shareholders with equal confidence in the ultimate reward of their spirited enterprise.

"The interest which the opening day attracted at the various stations on the line of road, as well as in the towns contiguous to them, was evidenced by the great number of persons who travelled by the trains, and by the immense multitudes who flocked to witness their passing, and testified their admiration of the ease and rapidity of this mode of transit by loud cheers.

"Every bridge, too, on, or rather across, the line was thronged with spectators on foot and in vehicles, whose countenances bore evident sign of astonishment at the velocity with which the ponderous machines shot through the arches.

"The fineness of the day contributed very considerably to add to the interest of the scene, and heightened the beauty of the surrounding country, which seemed like a splendid panorama, especially when crossing the viaduct at Hanwell, at which place a vast number of persons were collected, whose shouts, as the trains passed, were rapidly lost to the ear."

The 19-mile return journey from Salt Hill took 34 minutes. Board member Thomas Guppy, one of the Bristol pioneers, distinguished himself in a rather dubious manner by walking over the roofs of the carriages from end to end of the train while it was in motion. He became, in effect, the world's first 'train surfer' to cite an activity undertaken by some irresponsible youngsters today.

The first Maidenhead station was the western terminus of the GWR for just over a year, but was not situated in the town itself, for the great railway bridge spanning the Thames had yet to be built. Built out of wood, the station was renamed Maidenhead & Taplow in August 1854 and just plain Taplow on November 1, 1871.

It was closed on September 1, 1872, when the existing Taplow station was opened a quarter of a mile to the east, although it is a considerable distance south of the village from which it takes its name.

A BRIDGE NOT TOO FAR

While Wharncliffe viaduct was magnificent, as far as young Isambard was concerned the Victorians had not seen anything yet.

At Maidenhead, Brunel was faced with crossing the 100ft-wide Thames, a busy inland waterway where the river commissioners would not allow any obstruction to endanger the barge traffic — which the GWR eventually killed off.

He was allowed just one single support in the middle of the river. In return, Brunel had his own stipulation. He stoutly refused to deviate from the markedly smooth and gentle 1-in-1320 ruling gradient between Paddington and Didcot by raising the height of the line to cross the river. Indeed, his GWR main line east of Swindon was so flat that it earned the nickname of 'Brunel's billiard table'.

The answer was to come up with a new type of bridge, the like of which the world had not seen before. The result was a bridge, now Grade I listed, which carries the railway across the river on two brick arches. When they were built these were the widest and flattest in the world. It crosses the Thames on the reach between Bray Lock and Boulter's Lock at the downstream end of Guards Club Island.

The biggest brick feature on the London-Bristol line, each span is 128ft, with a rise of only 24ft — essential if a hump in the middle was to be avoided. The right-hand arch is known as the Sounding Arch, because of its impressive echo.

Critics said it could not be done and that the arches would collapse. It has been said that GWR directors also did not believe they would hold firm under the weight of the trains and that they told Brunel to leave the wooden formwork used to construct them in place. The wily Isambard simply lowered the formwork slightly so that it had no structural effect, although it looked to be in place.

The formwork was later washed away in floods, but the bridge held fast, proving Brunel right. It is still in use by today's high-speed trains, and will be fitted with masts when the line is electrified.

Isambard later admitted, however, that had it been built 20 years later, he would have used cast iron or timber for the bridge.

Maidenhead Bridge features in J M W Turner's 1844 painting Rain, Steam and Speed — The Great Western Railway, which can be seen in the National Gallery in London.

Completed in 1838, the bridge was not brought into use until July 1, 1839, when the railway was extended westwards to Twyford, 31 miles from Paddington, from where a branch was later built to Henley-on-Thames.

ONWARDS TO READING

In the first year, the GWR carried 606,396 passengers. It was extended to Reading in 1840. Locomotive *Fire Fly*, the first of a world-beating class of 2-2-2s, proudly headed a special directors' train from Paddington to Reading on March 14, 1840, prior to the first public services running on March 30.

Faster progress was not made because laying Brunel's broad gauge track took longer than a 'normal' standard railway gauge with sleepers. The 30ft 'baulks' laid between each cross-member at 15ft intervals and packed with ballast to form a firm foundation for the base used far more manpower and raw materials. This system of laying track, and indeed, its design, was not adopted elsewhere in Britain, because it was so labour intensive.

Brunel designed both Reading and Slough stations as one sided. He took the view that the entrance and booking hall should be on the side of the railway where the town lay so that the public should not have to cross the tracks.

The eastbound (Up) and westbound (Down) platforms were built on the same side, and each accessed by loops off the main line. Trains had to cross over to access the platforms to pick up or set down passengers — rather than the passengers doing the legwork. That was not a problem in the early days when traffic was sparse, but as soon as it intensified, bottle-necks arose.

In the meantime, Brunel thought that the idea was working well, and repeated the arrangement at other stations, including Taunton, Gloucester, Newton Abbot and Exeter.

Eventually, to cope with rising volume of traffic the one-sided stations were replaced, and Reading became the last to be converted, in 1899, with Up, Down and relief platforms linked by a pedestrian subway.

When Reading station opened as a temporary western terminus, the time taken to travel from London to Reading was cut to one hour and five minutes, less than a quarter of the time taken by the fastest stagecoach. The iron horse was fast replacing the equine version.

The station was the scene of one of the first railway accidents on the GWR, but it did not involve a train.

While building work on the station was nearing completion on March 24, 1840, workman Henry West, 24, was on top of the station when what was described at the time as a tornado lifted that section of the roof. The wind carried it and West around 20ft, the fall killing him outright. A brass plaque on the wall of the main station building commemorates the freak event.

The Great Western Hotel, thought to be the oldest surviving railway hotel building in the world, was opened in 1844. Known as the Malmaison Hotel since 2007, some think that Brunel had a hand in its design — including English Heritage.

Reading went on to become an important junction in its own right, with the line from Reading to Newbury and Hungerford opening in 1847, and the line to Basingstoke in 1848. A new Bath Stone station building, complete with a tower and clock, was built in 1860. Originally named Reading, the station became Reading General on September 26, 1949, in order to differentiate it from the ex-South Eastern Railway station nearby.

The GWR built a small engine shed in the junction of the lines to Didcot and those to Basingstoke in 1841. It was enlarged and rebuilt in 1876 and again in 1930, but was closed by British Railways in 1965 and replaced by the existing Traction Maintenance Depot.

DIGGING THE GREAT CUTTING

Beyond Reading, a great obstacle lay in the path of the GWR — Sonning Hill at Holme Park. Brunel had originally thought of burrowing a mile-long tunnel to the north of the hill to appease the local landowner who objected to the railway being an eyesore, but directors feared that passengers might be too scared to ride through it so Isambard ordered a massive cutting to be dug.

During summer 1838, a team of 1200 navvies using 200 horses excavated the gigantic trench by hand, using picks and shovels. Several people died in the process.

The project took until the end of 1839 to complete, having been plagued by poor weather during the previous winter. Where the slopes of the hill had blocked the way, there was now Sonning Cutting, which was nearly two miles long and up to 60ft deep.

A court case began in the wake of the collapse of contractors who had been appointed to dig the cutting. The legal proceedings lasted a marathon 17 years before final judgement was given.

A brick three-arch bridge was built to take the main London-Reading road across the cutting, along with a smaller timber bridge that is thought to have been a precursor for Brunel's great trestle viaducts that he later built in Devon and Cornwall.

The cutting was the scene of one of Britain's worst early railway accidents when a mixed goods and passenger luggage train hit debris from a landslide early on Christmas Eve 1841.

At the time, open-top wagons were still very much in service as passenger carriages and many riding in these were thrown out or crushed between the wagons. The train comprised Leo class 2-4-0 *Hecla*, which has been supplied by the Leeds firm of Fenton, Murray & Jackson eight months before, a tender, three third-class passenger carriages and some heavily-laden goods wagons. The passenger carriages were between the tender and the freight wagons and there were 38 people on board them.

Heavy rain had saturated the soil in the cutting, causing a slippage and covering the line on which the train was travelling. The engine was derailed shortly before 7am, causing rapid deceleration. The passenger coaches were then crushed between the goods wagons, which were thrown into the air, and the tender.

Eight people died in the accident and one afterwards in hospital, with another 16 injured. Some of the dead were artisans returning home after working on the new Parliament building. After being told about the crash, Brunel immediately left London with around 100 workmen aboard a special train to clear the soil from the line.

An inquiry jury returned a verdict of accidental death in all cases, and imposed a deodand of £1000 on the engine, tender, and carriages. A deodand is an object or instrument which becomes forfeit because it has caused someone death. The English common law principle existed from the 11th century. For instance, if a horse caused someone's death, a value was placed on it by a jury and the owner had to pay the sum of money. If he could not, his town would have to stump up. The money raised was supposed to be used for 'pious' means. The practice had largely fallen into disuse until the coming of the railways.

As the national network began to take shape, and speeds increased, the general public became hostile to the thought of railway accidents and deaths. As English law permitted no damages to be awarded to victims' families, coroner's juries began to get round the problem by invoking deodands. However, in the case of the Sonning Cutting crash, a Board of Trade inspector exonerated the company from blame and the deodand was quashed on appeal.

Despite much opposition from railway companies, Lord Campbell introduced a Bill in 1845 to compensate victims, leading to the Fatal Accidents Act 1846, and also one to abolish deodands, which the railways welcomed.

In the aftermath of the tragedy, William Ewart Gladstone, then President of the Board of Trade, brought in legislation to improve safety on the railways, in the form of the 1844 Railway Regulation Act requiring railway companies to provide better carriages for passengers.

HEADQUARTERS AT STEVENTON

The section from Reading to Steventon on the Oxford turnpike road opened on June 1, 1840, allowing the great university city 10 miles to the north to be reached by a road coach link. That arrangement lasted until it was superseded by a station at Didcot in 1844 — a case of an early park-and-ride. However, mail trains from the West continued to call at Steventon, rather than Didcot, in order to drop off mail for Oxford, until March 1962.

The line from Reading to Steventon crossed the Thames twice: at Basildon Bridge west of Pangbourne and Moulsford Viaduct just before Cholsey. Another classic structure, the 203ft span wrought-iron bowstring Thames Bridge, was built on the short branch from Slough to Windsor.

Engineer George Thomas Clark played a key role on this section of the line, including these two bridges with their sweeping brick arches. Anonymously, he wrote two guidebooks on the railway: one illustrated with lithographs by John Cooke Bourne, many of which are reproduced here. The other was a critique of Brunel's methods and his broad gauge.

Clark became a member of the Royal College of Surgeons in 1832 but in an abrupt career change was later employed by Brunel on the GWR, with overall responsibility for some stretches of the line and for civil structures. Later, from 1843-47, he worked on the Great Indian Peninsula Railway, surveying and planning the first passenger line in India, from Bombay to Thana, which was opened in 1852.

Near Steventon station, Brunel ordered a large Tudor house to be built for the line's superintendent. It was also used as the directors' offices and for their board meetings in the early years, and in effect therefore became for the time being the company's headquarters.

When the board decided to merge the previously separate London and Bristol committees in October 1841, Steventon was chosen as a suitable new location for weekly board meetings from July 21, 1842, because it was near the halfway point of the line — around 56 miles from Paddington and 61 miles from Bristol. The situation persisted until January 5, 1843, when permanent headquarters at Paddington were ready.

On December 7, 1964, British Railways withdrew passenger services from Steventon and all other intermediate stations between Didcot and Swindon, during the Beeching Axe. Eliminating stopping trains was a move designed to speed up traffic and make inter-city travel more attractive to the customer. Steventon station was demolished soon after closure, leaving no trace.

Services extended to Faringdon Road, 63½ miles from Paddington, on July 20, 1840. Faringdon Road, later renamed Challow, served as a temporary western terminus for five months.

On December 17, 1840, services were extended to Hay Lane, a minor road crossing at the entrance to Studley cutting, four miles from Wootton Bassett, and soon officially named Wootton Bassett Road. At this point, the GWR issued its first proper passenger timetable.

During the building of the railway, when it was not open throughout, basic locomotive facilities were provided at Wootton Bassett. Road coaches took passengers to and from Bath, where they could take a train on the completed section to Bristol. The GWR arranged with the coach proprietors for a fixed mileage rate.

There were three GWR stations serving Wootton Bassett over 125 years. The first, Wootton Bassett Road, was in use from 1840-41, and was superseded by Wootton Bassett station, which served the town until 1903. It was rebuilt as Wootton Bassett Junction when a new route to south Wales was opened, and new platforms with brick-built buildings were installed. The main offices and goods yard were in nearly the same places as before.

Two signal boxes, Wootton Bassett West and Wootton Bassett East, were brought into use. The station was closed in 1965.

From here, the line to the west had to cross the southern Cotswold Hills, and needed major earthworks which tested Brunel's design skills, beginning with a huge problematic incline at Wootton Bassett. Constant rain during the wet winter of 1839 caused landslips at many of the embankments built from the spoil which had been excavated from the cuttings built by his army of navvies. It has been said that there is hardly a length of line between Swindon and Bristol where the natural ground was used for the railway.

THE RAILWAY TOWN OF THE WEST

The name Swindon needs no introduction whatsoever in railway circles. Three miles back up the line from Wootton Bassett Road, it was a sleepy market town on the North Wilts Canal until the railway came — when Brunel elevated it to international fame.

By December 1840, the line had reached Swindon, which had been chosen as the junction for the broad gauge Cheltenham & Great Western Union Railway, an independent line worked by the GWR, which opened on May 13, 1841.

Swindon station was opened on July 17, 1842 on the existing site, and until 1961 was known as Swindon Junction. It was built by contractor J&C Rigby at its own expense in return for the right to operate the refreshment rooms on the ground floor and a hotel on the upper ones.

Indeed, this company even obtained an agreement from the GWR that all trains would stop there for 10 minutes so that refreshments could be bought. Locomotives were changed in the meantime.

These were the first recorded railway refreshment rooms and were divided according to class. Townsfolk were proud of the fact that royalty had used them but the remarkable stopping arrangement led to many complaints over the ensuing half century, with the GWR finally buying back the lease in 1895.

Legend has it that Brunel and his locomotive superintendent Daniel Gooch were surveying a vale north of Swindon Hill when they chose the town for the site of the GWR's central workshops. It was said Brunel either threw a stone or dropped a picnic sandwich and declared that spot to be the new location of the works.

The choice probably had more to do with the location of the canal, which in the days before a national railway network was established would bring in supplies of coal from the Somerset mines for the locomotives as well as basic building materials.

Also, because the terrain west of Swindon became more hilly than the 'billiard table' to Paddington, engines had to be changed because a different type of locomotive would be needed for the gradients.

The original station building was demolished in 1972, before the existing modern station and office block erected were built.

The section of the line from Wootton Bassett Road to Chippenham was opened on May 31, 1841. The first train from Paddington that day brought Brunel and senior company officials, and they were treated to a public breakfast by the town major and leading citizens.

Chippenham has one of the most attractive of all the station buildings on the line. Built from a deep rich yellowstone, it was not quite ready for the first day. Nonetheless, when opened, the station reduced the travelling time from Bath to London to five hours.

The writing had now been on the wall for the road coach operators for many months. After the spring of 1840, only one coach was left plying its trade between Bath and London without using the railway. It was also said that the once-prosperous coaching inn landlords along the Great West Road were starving because of the sudden drop in their incomes.

The original station building at Chippenham was designed by Brunel. Next to the wonderful Grade II listed yellowstone station booking office and entrance stands an office building, restored by Chippenham Civic Society, and which is believed to have been Isambard's office while he oversaw the building of this section of the route.

To the immediate south of Chippenham station, Brunel's 90-yard Cotswold stone Chippenham Viaduct, also known as the Western Arches, and which are also Grade II listed, overnight became one of the major landmarks of the town. The first arch, which spans New Road, seems to have been inspired by a Roman triumphal arch. Two smaller pedestrian arches sit either side of the 26ft span.

Chippenham was soon served by other lines, firstly the Wilts, Somerset & Weymouth Railway which ran from Thingley Junction to the west of the town to Westbury and which opened in stages from September 5, 1848, and the Calne Railway which opened on November 3, 1863. The original station building soon became inadequate to cope with growing numbers of passengers and was redesigned by J H Bertram during 1856-58.

Beyond Chippenham's viaduct, a two-mile embankment had to be built, before the line passed through Corsham in a deep three-mile cutting, to the eastern portal of Box Tunnel.

Work south of Chippenham began in summer 1837, but the winter of 1839 was particularly rainy and landslips were frequent, impeding progress.

CHAPTER FIVE

Building east from Bristol

BRISTOL TEMPLE Meads, not Paddington, was the first great terminus for Brunel and his Great Western Railway. Work on building the station began in 1839 and took two years to complete. The name Temple Meads comes from the nearby Temple Church, built by the Knights Templar, the great monastic order of medieval crusading warriors, in the 12th century, and 'mæds', Old English for meadows, plenty of which could be found alongside the River Avon. Indeed, what is a bustling site today was undeveloped pasture outside the boundaries of the old city in 1820, situated between the Floating Harbour and the city's cattle market, which was built in 1830.

Brunel was banned from building his station within the medieval walls of the city, so Temple Meads was the next best site. He built his station on a viaduct to raise it above the level of the Floating Harbour. It was built on the same scale as a cathedral and was completed 14 years before the GWR gave London a similar structure of the same size and prominence at Paddington.

The GWR's Bristol Committee had expressed dismay at the very basic original Paddington terminus and insisted that Isambard provide something far more grandiose. Brunel was only too pleased to provide it.

When completed, the timber and iron roof of the passenger shed formed the widest single span of the day, supported by 44 massive brick flattened arches, a 74ft single-span wooden hammerbeam roof, a copy of Westminster Hall, covered the 220ft-long trainshed and its five tracks.

The train shed was extended beyond the platforms by 155ft into a storage area and engine shed. The locomotive shed was fronted by a limestone ashlar office building in mock Tudor style to hide it. It included a boardroom and offices for the Bristol Committee.

At first, Temple Meads consisted of just an arrival and a departure platform. Hydraulic turntables in the engine shed were used to transfer the trains between tracks. Passengers moved between platforms through the undercroft, which contained the waiting rooms.

Train services to Bath began on August 31, 1840, 10 months before the entire line to Paddington was completed on June 30, 1841.

However, a few weeks before, on June 14, the Bristol & Exeter Railway had opened as far south as Bridgwater. At first it used the GWR station, with its trains reversing in and out via a curved line.

On July 8, 1844, the Bristol & Gloucester Railway, which had been initially built to broad gauge, entered Temple Meads, being taken over by the Midland Railway on July 1, 1845. It too used the GWR platforms, and on May 29, 1854, laid a third rail on the Bristol to Gloucester line to create mixed gauge, capable of handling both Brunel broad gauge and Stephenson standard gauge trains.

The Bristol & Exeter opened its own temporary station in 1845, at right angles to the GWR structure, following it up with a permanent one designed by Samuel Fripp in Jacobean style in 1854. As well as the Bristol & Exeter and Bristol & Gloucester, Brunel also designed the Bristol and South Wales Union Railway, which was completed on August 25, 1863, four years after his death. It also ran into Temple Meads.

As traffic levels rose, Temple Meads became outmoded, but it was not until 1865 that an Act of Parliament was obtained to rebuild it. Matthew Digby Wyatt produced a Gothic design, and building work on the new station began in 1871, with the first section of the station opening on July 6, 1874, and the finished station with all seven platforms on January 1, 1878.

Running eastwards from Temple Meads, the railway crosses a mile of arches, a larger one to take it over the Floating Harbour and then another, with a 100ft span, across the Avon. All of these were designed to a 15th-century style.

There were six tunnels on the Bristol to Bath stretch: Bristol No. 1 (326 yards) which had a Romanesque portal but was opened out into a cutting in 1889; Bristol No. 2, today known as St Anne's Tunnel (154 yards); Fox's Wood No. 3 (1017 yards); Saltford (176 yards) and Twerton Long Tunnel (264 yards), which has castellated portals, intended by Brunel to convey grandeur, and Twerton Short Tunnel (45 yards).

Fox's Wood No. 3 west portal was also to be castellated but the frontage collapsed during heavy rain. Brunel was delighted: he ordered it to be left as a romantic ivy-clad ruin, in accordance with the fashion of the day.

We have seen that Brunel surveyed his railway on horseback. However, there was at least one exception, when his solicitor Jeremiah Osborne of Bristol law firm Osborne Clarke rowed him down the Avon to survey the bank of the river for the route. Osborne Clarke was also appointed to represent the GWR, and today remains one of the biggest law firms in the UK in terms of revenue.

The next town served to the east of Bristol was Keynsham, renamed Keynsham & Somerdale on February 1, 1925 with the opening of the Fry's chocolate factory at Somerdale, and rebuilt in 1931. Sadly, the Tudor-style station buildings designed by Brunel were demolished in 1970, although the station is very much open and thriving with commuters. Beyond there was Saltford station — a small wooden structure which burned down in 1873 before it was replaced by stone. It closed to passengers on January 5, 1970.

While building Saltford Tunnel, navvies cut through a spring which supplied the village of Saltford with water. The authorities gave the GWR 21 days to rectify the matter, but water carts were used to supply houses in the village for several years afterwards. Further on lay Bath Twerton station, which was built in Gothic style to serve Twerton village, as it then was. It opened on December 16, 1840, but only four out of 11 services each way stopped there.

It was renamed Twerton-on-Avon in 1899 to avoid confusion with Tiverton, and was closed in 1917 as an economy measure during the First World War, succumbing to competition from an electric tram line which ran from Twerton to Bath city centre. In 1929, Oldfield Park station was opened nearby. Both the station building, which has seen a variety of uses since its closure, and the viaduct on which it sits are Grade II listed.

Two tunnels take the line through the Carrs Woodland hillside in Twerton; the bigger of them, Twerton Long Tunnel, has a castellated western portal designed to give passengers a sense of grandeur. The hillside above the tunnels is now the Carrs Woodland nature reserve.

In Regency Bath, there had been much opposition to the coming of the railway and Brunel had to work out the fine dividing line between bringing the GWR into the city while not ruining the richness of its historic areas.

Bath Spa station, a Grade II* listed building with a two-storey frontage on the north bank of the Avon, was designed by Brunel in an asymmetrical Tudor style with curving gables. Artistic merit had to be at the fore here, to provide a building that would fit in with the town so beloved by the likes of Jane Austen, rather than one that would stand out as an eyesore. A mock hammerbeam roof with a span of 6oft originally covered the area between the platforms, but it was removed in 1897. The booking office and other facilities lay in the basement.

The wide space between the tracks today is evidence that it was built to broad gauge standards; there was once a bi-directional line between the Up and Down tracks.

The railway crosses the Avon from the south bank before and after the station to reach it, with an acutely-skewed stone bridge on the Bristol side. As a result, while the southern side of the city ended up being dominated by railway viaducts and embankments, the centre's 18th-century splendour was left undisturbed. Originally named plain Bath, the station became Bath Spa in 1949 to differentiate it from the Somerset & Dorset terminus at Bath Green Park, which until 1951 was also simply called Bath.

The classical St James Bridge over the Avon is followed by a 32-arch viaduct across Dolemeads. St James Bridge, built on a skew, was one of the last works on this section of the railway to be completed. Work was well advanced by January 1841 when it was abruptly swept away by floods, and had to be built again from scratch.

The GWR was not Bath's first railway — that honour goes to a tramway which carried quarried stone from Combe Down to a wharf on the river in the 1720s. Its course is now occupied by Prior Park Road.

Beyond, there was another obstacle to overcome — not a mighty river to cross nor a great mass of earth to tunnel or cut through, but one which required no less ingenuity. The 'predecessor' to the railway, the Kennet & Avon Canal, stood in the way. A section of the canal at Sydney Gardens, a Bath pleasure park, needed to be diverted.

It was no easy task — for anyone but Isambard Kingdom Brunel. He defied all expectations and devised a 27ft high retaining wall which was up to 5ft thick, thereby creating a barrier between his railway cutting and the canal. Various garden features and buildings were destroyed including a tea house, part of a labyrinth, a castle, and the 18th-century perimeter walk. However, Brunel deliberately improved the appearance of the gardens by building one stone and one ornamental cast-iron bridge to link the two parts of the park which had been bisected by both railway and canal. Furthermore, he built a skewed stone bridge to carry Sydney Road.

His railway soon became the biggest attraction of all in the pleasure grounds as groups of people gathered to watch the passing trains. Because of the poor state of Bath station in 1881, the Sydney Gardens section of the railway was chosen as the disembarkation point for a visit by the Duke and Duchess of Connaught.

CHAPTER SIX

The legend that is Box Tunnel

T HERE WERE two Great Western Railways in operation by 1840, one running from London to Chippenham and the other from Bristol to Bath. Isambard Kingdom Brunel now faced his biggest hurdle of all in order to join the two together.

Standing in the way of his route was an outlier of the Cotswolds called Box Hill. He had a plan, but it would push his design and engineering skills to the limit and resulted in the deaths of around 100 navvies — a cost that would be unthinkable today.

The plan was to push a 1.83-mile tunnel through the solid Bath stone hill. Critics said that this proposal was unworkable. According to one MP, the necessary 1-in-100 gradient was so great that if a train's brakes failed, it would go out of control in the blackness — leaving the tunnel at 120mph. Doctors raised fears that passengers would suffocate in the steam, warning that nobody would be able to survey two journeys through the tunnel.

During a marathon 57-day parliamentary hearing on the plans to build the GWR, none other than George Stephenson was called as a witness for the railway. Under cross examination, he was told by counsel: "The noise of two trains passing each other in this tunnel would shake the nerves of this assembly. I do not know such a noise. No passenger would be induced to go twice."

Again, as with the issues of broad gauge and Maidenhead Bridge, Brunel paid no heed. He wanted only the best railway of them all, and nothing, least of all a stubborn hill, would get in his way. Work on the tunnel began in September 1836, about a year after the railway had been given parliamentary assent. Between 1836 and 1837, eight shafts were sunk at intervals through the hill and along the projected alignment to establish the nature of the underlying rock, which largely comprised great oolite limestone (Bath stone) and inferior oolite, Fuller's earth and a small amount of Lias clay. Supervising this work was Charles Richardson, who was later responsible for the GWR's Severn Tunnel.

Overseen by Brunel and resident engineer William Glennie, two contractors were appointed to construct the tunnel: George Burge from Herne Bay was responsible for 75% of the overall length working from the west, and locally based Lewis & Brewer undertook the rest.

Boring the tunnel began in December 1838, and the scheme involved 1500 men, rising to 4000 at Brunel's insistence as the tunnel neared completion, working in shifts day and night. Labourers shared beds in the nearby villages of Box and Corsham; as one got out to go to work, another came home and took his place. As was the case with mass gatherings of railway navvies elsewhere in Britain, there were frequent bouts of drunkenness and disorder in the locality, including fights between rival gangs of navvies, while the tunnel was being built.

For example, it was recorded that on August 18, 1839, labourer William Vickers died in the Chequers Inn near Corsham after drinking too much beer, gin and ginger beer.

A team of 100 horses was used to take away the 247,000 cubic yards of material, including hundreds of thousands of tons of spoil, some of which was used to build the Railway Village in Swindon, housing workers at the great locomotive works which was taking shape. The construction was split into six isolated sections, accessed at first only through the 25ft diameter ventilation shafts, which ranged in depth from 70ft to 300ft. Around a ton of gunpowder and candles were used each week. Workmen often had to flee for their lives as water broke through from the great oolite strata.

The excavations from the ends of the tunnel finally met in spring 1841. Isambard's calculations had been so accurate that the side walls lined up within an inch and a half. When this was apparent, Isambard was so delighted that he took a ring off his finger and gave it to the workman who stood next to him.

Brunel designed a grand classical portal for the west end of the tunnel, one of the most visually striking pieces of infrastructure on any railway in Britain, or elsewhere for that matter. Indeed, a hallmark of his genius was an ability not only to push technology to its limits but also to finesse the end product with artistic excellence. Sadly, so many engineers who came after him opted for basic functional and utilitarian structures. However, the eastern portal of Box Tunnel is less flamboyant, with simple stonework.

Isambard boasted that the tunnel, at 9636ft with a 25ft diameter bore, was the longest in Britain. It was indeed the longest railway tunnel at the time, but its length was exceeded by the 11,541ft Sapperton Tunnel on the Thames & Severn Canal which had been finished half a century before. By June 30, 1841, one of the two tracks was ready so that trains could pass through the tunnel. It opened without any ceremony whatsoever on that day.

The first through train was a directors' special which left Paddington at 8am and arrived in Bristol four hours later. Who then would ever again spend several days making the journey by stagecoach?

The earlier fears of the critics, however, were not entirely disproved at the outset. Some travellers who suffered from claustrophobia or who feared that the air pressure inside would be dangerous left the train before the tunnel and rejoined it on the other side, having made a round journey by road. Indeed, the 18-room Railway Hotel was established at Corsham for those who chose not to go through the tunnel, but in this respect it did not prove a commercial success.

GWR directors suggested lighting the tunnel, but Brunel was against the idea, saying that it was no darker than the rest of his railway at night.

With the opening of the tunnel, trains could run not only straight through from Paddington to Bristol, but also all 152 miles to Bridgwater, as building of the Bristol & Exeter Railway was by then well advanced. That is what the VIP train on the first day did — leaving Paddington at 8am, arriving at Bristol at 12pm and reaching Bridgwater at 1.30pm. The first public train left Bristol at 7am.

Around 100 flags decorated the grandiose western portal of Box Tunnel and the road bridge a short distance away. A band played, and around 1200 pints of beer were given away.

The first locomotive through the tunnel on the day was Sun class 2-2-2 *Meridian* and Brunel stood beside driver Cuthbert Davison. The critics were wrong: nobody ever suffocated in the tunnel and high-speed trains regularly use it today. It will enter a new phase in its history when electric overhead wires are installed throughout.

A myth arose that the rising sun shines through Box Tunnel on Brunel's birthday on April 9. This is not the case, although the sun does shine directly through the tunnel on other days in April and September.

FROM BRUNEL TO THE COLD WAR

A major spin-off from the excavation of the tunnel was huge supplies of Bath stone, a superb building material. After the tunnel was completed, enterprising locals began quarrying adjacent parts of Box Hill for more supplies of this very attractive stone. Eventually, the hill became riddled with a labyrinth of quarries and passages serving them.

Nearby Corsham became a boom town as the stone was mined and quarried, with nearly 1000 people engaged in the industry by late Victorian times, the stone being taken out by the GWR through a standard gauge freight branch running directly off the main line at the eastern portal of Box Tunnel into the great underground caverns.

By 1943, Corsham's Central Ammunition Depot, as it became known, was the focal point of 125 acres of subterranean chambers containing 300,000 tons of explosives and munitions, not only in the caverns near Box Tunnel but in separate underground quarries throughout the Bath region.

The freight spur from the tunnel portal into the 50-acre Tunnel Quarry was upgraded for military use. Complete with a 750ft underground platform and refuge sidings, it ran for around 2000ft underground. Inside the caverns, it led to a 2ft gauge internal railway system with its own diesel locomotives, turntables, engine houses and workshops serving the gigantic ammunition store, which was divided into 'districts'.

Three Hunslet 0-6-0 diesel shunters, chosen because they would not emit sparks in the ammunition dump, worked the standard gauge line, taking wagons to and from the reception sidings at the GWR's Thingley Junction three miles away. Daily maintenance of the locomotives was conducted at the underground locomotive shed.

Whitehall spread rumours that the Ministry of Food was building an emergency food dump to cover up the real purpose of the caverns. At the outbreak of the Second World War, many RAF command centres were located underground. An RAF station was established using one area of the tunnels: RAF Box. No. 10 Fighter Command was housed in Brown's Quarry, an offshoot of Tunnel Quarry. In 1940, the extensive Spring Quarry, on the other side of Brunel's tunnel from Tunnel Quarry, was converted by the Ministry of Aircraft Production into what was described as "the largest underground factory in the world" where the Bristol Aeroplane Company turned out Centaurus engines.

A separate part was used by BSA for making gun barrels. However, by the time these shadow factories opened in early 1943, bombing raids by the Luftwaffe were a much diminished threat. Yet the £20 million spent on adapting the caverns would not be wasted and the network of quarries became a focal point of Cold War planning.

On August 29, 1949, the Soviet Union tested its first fission bomb, nicknamed Joe 1 by the USA. The western world was shocked at how much further ahead the USSR was in its nuclear weapons research than had previously been thought. Soviet Premier Nikita Khrushchev delivered a speech in November 1958 in which he insisted that the USA, United Kingdom and France pull their forces out of West Berlin within six months. His demand started a three-year crisis over the future of Berlin that led to the building of the Berlin Wall in 1961.

October 1962 saw the world teeter on the brink of a nuclear holocaust as the USA challenged the USSR in the Cuban missile crisis. Originally codenamed Subterfuge, the Corsham caverns, including over 60 miles of internal roads and covering 35 acres, 100ft below the town, were subsequently converted into an office for prime minister Harold Macmillan, the war cabinet and chiefs of staff, and possibly the royal family.

It was said that the complex — known as Burlington — could house up to 4000 central Government staff. A New York grid-style city of roads and avenues was equipped with all the facilities essential for survival; everything from underground hospitals, laboratories, canteens, kitchens and laundries to storerooms of supplies, accommodation areas, offices and a bar.

An underground lake and treatment plant was installed to provide all the drinking water needed while 12 huge tanks could store the fuel required to keep four massive generators in the underground power station running for three months.

The underground city also had the second largest telephone exchange in Britain and a BBC studio from which the prime minister could address the nation. Many of the civil servants who had, unbeknown to them, been allocated a desk there knew nothing whatsoever about the existence of the city, such was the veil of secrecy that enshrouded it.

The Emergency Government War Headquarters, as it was designated, was last upgraded in the early years of the Thatcher government, when the USSR invaded Afghanistan. However, the fall of communism and the break-up of the Soviet Union made the bunker city obsolete. By then down to just four staff, in December 2008, the underground site was finally decommissioned, much of it being sold off or used for commercial storage, although an RAF and military communications base remains. The entrance from Box Tunnel is now bricked up.

STRATEGIC RESERVE

For many years legends persisted among parts of the railway enthusiast fraternity that following the end of British Railways steam in 1968, many locomotives had been buried beneath Salisbury Plain as a 'strategic reserve'. It was said that they would be unearthed in the event of a global crisis when diesel fuel was in short supply or when the detonation of a nuclear bomb had wiped out the electronic circuits needed to make diesel locomotives operate.

Three men entered Box Tunnel in September 2003 seeking the entrance and landed themselves in court after causing six-hour delays to main line services while they were rescued.

There were never any old steam engines concealed inside the city, but the conspiracy theorists were not entirely wrong. Among the disused underground offices and stores was left one 2ft gauge Hunslet four-wheeled diesel, WD1, which ran on the internal system.

Had Brunel taken another route for his railway, would the underground city have ever been built there?

THE ROUTE COMPLETED

Cutting the journey time from London to Bath and Bristol by several days to four hours was literally *Rocket* science back in 1841. The Stephensons' famous locomotive of that name, the Liverpool & Manchester Railway's flagship when it opened in 1830, was a defining image of a period in which the world's approach to long-distance transport was changing forever.

The entire 116-mile Great Western Railway from Paddington to Bristol Temple Meads was opened throughout on June 30, 1841, with the completion of the biggest hurdle of them all, Box Tunnel. By that date, other lines were linking into Brunel's first main line, and railways were not only giving Bristol a link to the capital but also pushing further south, towards Exeter and beyond.

It had been eight-and-a-half years since the first meeting of the Bristol railway committee in January 1833 saw the appointment of Brunel, then aged just 27. Would a project of such magnitude be trusted to someone so young today?

It was not, of course, all plain sailing for Brunel. In 1839, alarmed at rising costs, GWR shareholders tried in vain to remove Brunel from his position. Had they succeeded, what course would the railway have taken under a less adventurous engineer? There probably never would have been a Box Tunnel.

In marvelling at the magnificence of Brunel's structures, the loss of life among those who built them is so often overlooked. The death of 100 navvies at Box Tunnel, for instance, would have been a scandal of seismic proportions today, but in a world where the owning of slaves had still been legal until a few years before, life at lower levels of society was visibly cheaper than today.

Nonetheless, Brunel's big railway had even bigger implications for world history, showing just what could be achieved.

Prior to the Government's announcement that the line would be electrified — something of which Brunel almost certainly had approved — 56 structures were listed by English Heritage as being of special architectural or historic interest at a national level.

Following a review of the other structures along the route and adjacent lines carried out in conjunction with Network Rail in 2012, a further 35 were listed. The 2012 survey has ensured that, in advance of electrification, all heritage assets which deserve protection on a national scale have been identified and can then be appropriately managed through the planning process.

THE COMPLETION OF THE GWR

SECTION	DATE OPENED
1. Paddington to Maidenhead	June 4, 1838
2. Maidenhead to Twyford	July 1, 1839
3. Twyford to Reading	March 30, 1840
4. Reading to Steventon	June 1, 1840
5. Steventon to Challow	July 20, 1840
6. Bristol to Bath	August 31, 1840
7. Challow to Hay Lane	December 17, 1840
8. Hay Lane to Chippenham	May 31, 1841
9. Chippenham to Bath	June 30, 1841

CHAPTER SEVEN

The iron shire horses

NOBODY DOUBTS that Isambard Kingdom Brunel was one of the greatest engineers of the Victorian age. He repeatedly ripped up the rule book to produce stations, bridges, tunnels and cuttings that were years ahead of his day.

Yet when it came to choosing steam locomotives for his new breed of broad gauge railway, Isambard floundered badly. He ordered a total of 19 locomotives and to cut a long story short, most of them were barely fit for purpose.

Most successful of all was *North Star*, built by Robert Stephenson & Co and delivered by barge to Maidenhead Bridge on November 28, 1837. On May 31, 1838, it hauled the inaugural train for the GWR's directors. It was rebuilt in 1854 with the wheelbase lengthened by a foot, and after it was withdrawn in 1871 it was preserved at Swindon until 1906.

A similar locomotive, *Morning Star*, arrived from Stephenson & Co 14 months later. Its 6ft 6in driving wheels were 6in smaller than those of *North Star*, because it had been built to a cancelled order for the New Orleans Railway. Both locomotives gave the GWR sterling service, but far less successful were six Mather Dixon 2-2-2s chosen by Brunel.

The first of them, *Premier,* was delivered by canal to West Drayton on

November 25, 1837. It was followed by *Ariel, Ajax, Planet, Mars* and *Mercury*.

Planet entered service in 1839, but was withdrawn the following year, becoming a stationary boiler at Reading. *Mars* lasted in service only from April until December 1840. It had been delivered with 10ft driving wheels, which were changed to 8ft before it ran.

When *Premier* was delivered, it was accompanied by *Vulcan*, the first of three 2-2-2s built by Charles Tayleur at Vulcan Foundry of Newton-le-Willows, County Durham.

It became the first to run on the Great Western Railway when it was tested on December 28, 1837, from its shed at West Drayton. It was withdrawn in 1843 and rebuilt as a 2-2-2T, re-entering service in 1846 and lasting until 1868, before spending two years at Reading, also as a stationary boiler.

The second Charles Tayleur engine, *Æolus*, was delivered on November 30, 1837, and worked the first public train on the GWR when it opened to the public on June 4, 1838, but made a poor start on the day. In 1843, its driving wheels were changed from 8ft to 6ft and it was also rebuilt like *Vulcan*. Withdrawn in April 1867, it survived as a stationary boiler at Gloucester until July 1870.

The identical *Bacchus* was delivered on December 2, 1837, and from the outset was beset by breakdowns and abnormal wear and tear. It was withdrawn as early as June 1842 and sold around three years later.

Then there were three more Charles Tayleur locomotives. First was the *Apollo*, which was also converted to a 2-2-2T, and ran until August 1867, and sister *Neptune*, which lasted in service until only June 1840 and was scrapped five years later. A third of this type was *Venus*, delivered on September 7, 1838. It ran until 1843, when it was withdrawn and also changed into a 2-2-2T. Withdrawn again in July 1870, the boiler was used at Swindon as a stationary engine for several years.

Brunel also ordered two unusual Haigh Foundry locomotives, *Snake* and *Viper* with geared driving wheels to keep the cylinder stroke speed low while allowing high track speed, in line with Brunel's specifications. Both were extensively modified and later converted to 2-2-2Ts, running until the late 1860s.

Most bizarre were a pair from R&W Hawthorn & Co, Newcastle, which had the engine and boiler on separate frames. *Thunderer*, an 0-4-0, was delivered March 6, 1838. The boiler stood on a separate six-wheel frame attached behind the engine.

It was useless as a design, having no adhesive weight and requiring excessive amounts of coke to operate. It was withdrawn in December 1839 with 9882 miles on the clock. The engine was sold, but the boiler was reused for use as a stationary engine. *Hurricane*, a 2-2-2, delivered October 6, 1838, fared little better, lasting until December 1839 after travelling 10,527 miles. The boiler and some of the engine parts are thought to have been reused in 1849 for *Bacchus*, a new 0-6-0 freight engine. The most successful of the early types were three 2-2-2s, *Lion, Atlas* and *Eagle*, built by Sharp Roberts, and which lasted into the 1870s.

These engines had been designed and built to Brunel's own specifications but they did not correlate with his 'super railway' vision – and he realised that in the field of locomotive engineering, he just might be out of his depth.

ENTER DANIEL GOOCH

The Bristol committee had given young Isambard a golden opportunity when he was still in his 20s. He repaid the favour when, in 1837, he appointed his first locomotive superintendent – who was just 21. Daniel Gooch was born in Bedlington, Northumberland, on August 24, 1816. As a young boy he met George Stephenson and as soon as he was old enough, Daniel became an engineer at the locomotive works owned by Stockton & Darlington Railway promoter Edward Pease and Robert Stephenson.

After a stint at the foundry at Tredegar Ironworks in South Wales, he came to the notice of Isambard. Despite his tender years, Brunel was more than willing to take a gamble on him, having been suitably impressed. Young Daniel was plunged in at the deep end – having to find solutions to the problems with the first batches of imported locomotives and ensure that at least some of them could haul trains.

North Star was deemed to be not as efficient as it might be, and Brunel and Gooch worked together to successfully improve the steaming and reduce coke consumption. By increasing the size of the blast pipe and ensuring that the exhaust steam was discharged up the middle of the chimney, *North Star's* performance improved to the stage where it could haul a load of 40 tons at 40mph, using 33% less coke than previously.

Improvement work on *North Star* and its sister locomotives led to Gooch designing a class of his own. He would do for steam locomotive technology what Brunel had been doing for infrastructure. These were the days of huge copper domes, stovepipe chimneys, boilers shielded with wooden planks, a lack of cab roofs or weatherboarding to protect drivers and firemen, and gigantic central driving wheels. The bigger they were, the faster the engine would go, on Brunel's big railway. If the railway locomotive was to be known as the 'iron horse', these were the biggest breed of all — the cart or shire horses.

Gooch shared Isambard's deep conviction that 7ft 0¼in was a superior gauge and the real future of railways, because of greater safety, speed, luxury and capacity. A total of 62 examples of Gooch's Firefly class 2-2-2s were built by seven different outside manufacturers over two years.

The first, named *Fire Fly*, was built by Jones, Turner & Evans of Newton-le-Willows. Delivered on March 12, 1840, it made its debut 13 days later, hauling two carriages with 40 passengers on board and a truck from Paddington to Reading. It reportedly covered the 30¾miles from Twyford to Paddington in 37 minutes, an average speed of 50mph. Back in 1840, such speeds were unheard of.

Sister locomotive *Fire Ball* headed the first train from Bristol to Bath, on August 31, 1840. Gooch, who could drive engines as well as design them, was given the honour of driving the first Royal Train in 1842, hauled by his locomotive *Phlegethon*.

The Firefly class engines had chocolate-brown frames, green wheels with black tyres, vermillion buffer beams and a green boiler and firebox. This livery evolved into the famous Brunswick green which became the distinctive house style of the GWR empire right up until the end of steam, and which, following nationalisation in 1948, was adopted by British Railways for many of its locomotives built elsewhere.

Trials between broad and standard gauge engines took place during 1845 in a bid to decide which system was the best. Firefly class engine

Ixion exceeded 60mph and ran from London to Didcot with a 71 ton load at nearly 55mph, far superior to what standard gauge counterparts could offer. Fireflys were used on the postal trains between Paddington and Bristol introduced from February 1, 1855.

Class members ran in service for around half a million miles each, and when they were superseded by newer designs, many were converted to saddle tanks. The last Firefly, *Ixion*, was taken out of traffic in July 1879.

Gooch followed up the Firefly class in 1842 with his 21 Sun class 2-2-2s, built by four different outside makers. With 6ft rather than 7ft driving wheels, they were not as successful as the Fireflys, and were later rebuilt as saddle tanks.

After them came the Leo class 2-4-0s, which numbered 18, and which comprised the GWR's first purpose-built goods engines. The first GWR 0-6-0s were delivered in 1842, giving the company a fleet of 136 engines supplied by 11 different manufacturers.

By this stage, and probably long before, Gooch saw only too clearly that the way ahead for the expanding broad gauge network was to build its own engines, rather than buy them in. Brunel agreed. It was just a matter of choosing the site.

His original plan envisaged the GWR cutting through Savernake Forest near Marlborough. However, landowner the Marquess of Ailesbury objected. Brunel then redrew his plan, moving the railway 20 miles to the north, crossing the North Wilts Canal at the little market town of Swindon.

SWINDON: A BYWORD FOR EXCELLENCE

The popular legend as to how Swindon was chosen as the site for the GWR workshops was related in Chapter 4 but the following letter, written by Gooch to Brunel on September 13, 1840, throws more light on what really happened.

"My Dear Sir,

According to your wish I give you my views of the best site for our principal engine establishment, and in doing so I have studied the convenience of the Great Western Railway only, but also think the same point is the only place adapted for the Cheltenham and Great Western. The point I refer to is the junction at Swindon of the two lines. The only objection I see to Swindon is the bad supply of water. There is also an apparent inequality of distance or duty for the engines to work — but which is very much equalized when the circumstances attending it are taken into account. I find the actual distances are as 76½ to 41 miles and the gradients are for the short distance of 41 miles a rise of 318ft or 7.75ft per mile, and for the 76½ miles a rise of 292ft or 3.8ft per mile. Swindon being the point at which these gradients change, the different gradients necessarily require a different class of engine, requiring for the Bristol end a more powerful one than for the London end.

That power can only be obtained conveniently by reducing the diameter of the driving wheels, therefore, supposing we work between Swindon and Bristol with 6ft wheels, and between Swindon and London with 7ft wheels, there will actually be very little difference between the work required of the two engines, when the additional gradients and curves, and the increased number of revolutions per mile which the small wheeled engine makes are taken into account.

It would also divide the pilot engines very nearly equally, as Reading being the first station where a pilot engine would be kept, say 36 miles, the next distance, to Swindon, would then be 41 miles, and on to Bristol another 41, and which I think would be sufficiently near for pilot engines to be constantly ready, and with this arrangement the watering stations would work very well.

Steventon where plenty of water can be had, forming a central station between Reading and Swindon, and as our Oxford traffic comes on there I should think it likely that all trains will stop there.

A large station at Swindon would also enable us to keep our bank engines for Wootton Bassett incline at Swindon instead of having a separate station for that purpose at the bottom of the incline, and in addition it would at any rate be necessary to have a considerable station at Swindon to work the Cheltenham line, which would be saved if Swindon was our principal station.

It also has the great advantage of being on the side of a canal communicating with the whole of England, and by which we could get coal and coke, I should think at a moderate price. I am not sufficiently acquainted with the place to know how far we would be affected by the want of water, it might probably be collected in the neighbourhood, and as we have a great deal of side cutting they might be converted into reservoirs, and should even this fail us we have the canal.

These reasons lead me to think Swindon by far the best point we have for a central engine station. From the plans and sections there appear little or no difficulties with the nature of the ground for building upon, and by placing the station somewhere as shown in the enclosed sketch, it might be made in every respect very complete.

I have not thought of the Bristol & Exeter line in the arrangement, as it is quite possible to work it very well by engines kept at Bristol as long as they are fit for work.

In the same way we could work the additional Bath traffic, for when necessary they could always work their way to Swindon when any heavy repairs were required. The engine house we are building at Bristol would be ample for any slight repairs that might be required during the time the engine was in working order, and that without any outlay of machinery beyond a few hundred pounds. I am not aware of any difficulties connected with Swindon more than the water.

I am, my dear sir, yours very truly,
Daniel Gooch"

After visiting the greenfield site as indicated by Gooch, Brunel readily agreed that it should become the railway's engineering base. Building of the new works began in spring 1841, while housing was erected for the workforce, who would rapidly swell the population of the little country town.

The locomotive repair shed was the first building to be completed. It was equipped with machinery by 1842, the year that the town's station opened half a mile away.

J&C Rigby, the same enterprising company which successfully negotiated the refreshment room operation at Swindon station, built 300 cottages along with a railway hotel, in a housing estate that became known as New Swindon. Ever conscious of the soaring cost of building Brunel's big railway, Great Western directors agreed to reimbursement from tenants' rents.

New Swindon, one of the earliest examples of planned industrial housing in Britain, was originally separate from the town, but as the population grew, the green fields dividing the pair disappeared under bricks and mortar. It is today known as the Railway Village.

Designed by Sir Matthew Digby Wyatt, the architect of the Paddington station which replaced the original terminus, the Railway Village comprised 300 limestone-built terraced houses. Much of the stone came from the excavations of the Box Tunnel. Each home had its own small front garden, and the estate was designed with six tree-lined wide parallel streets named after GWR stations, with a central square. The bigger houses became homes to the under managers and foremen.

The village had three pubs and a church — St Mark's — with a school for the children of railway employees next door. There was a 10½ acre park for the recreation of the GWR workers and their families and at the heart of the village was the Mechanics' Institute, which opened on May 1, 1855, funded by Gooch and works manager Minard Christian Rea's New Swindon Improvement Company. It was intended to provide evening classes for manual workers and their families. There was a library, a theatre and stage, baths and coffee rooms, not to mention a marketplace in the Railway Village so that workers could buy fresh produce at reasonable prices. Gooch also recruited a works doctor who had free board and lodging.

Two centuries ago, life for the labouring classes was harsh, and life expectancy in the manufacturing cities and towns which mushroomed in the wake of the Industrial Revolution was nothing like that of today.

The slave trade had ended but young children still worked in factories and mines and as chimneysweeps. The conditions offered to railway workers and their families at Swindon were at worst futuristic, and showed that not only were the likes of Brunel and Gooch great technological innovators, but in accepting the principle that workers performed better if their living conditions were good, were also blazing a trail for social standards.

Works manager Archibald Sturrock declared the workshops to be in full operation in January 1843. The works included an engine depot built parallel to the main running line and which was capable of housing 100 locomotives. Next to it, at right angles, was the engine house, which could hold as many as 36 locomotives undergoing repairs and maintenance at any one time. On the north side of the engine house stood the erecting shop, capable of building 18 locomotives simultaneously.

Smaller workshops were built for pattern making, wheel turning, mill-wrights, tool making and copper work. The first repairs were undertaken in 1843 and at the start the workforce comprised 200. This had more than doubled by the end of the year to 423.

Premier, an 0-6-0 freight locomotive, the first of a class of a dozen engines, was assembled at the erecting shop in February 1846. However, it was not a true Swindon pedigree, as the boiler had been built elsewhere.

GREAT WESTERN PAVED THE WAY

The first all-Swindon-built locomotive was appropriately named *Great Western*. A 2-2-2, it looked like a Firefly but was an improvement on the design. At the time, the GWR was coming under increased political pressure to justify its use of broad gauge when the rest of Britain was running on 4ft 8½in, and responded by telling Gooch to come up with a 'colossal locomotive working with all speed' to show everyone just what Brunel's big railway could do.

Outshopped in April 1846 after just three months, *Great Western* was a world beater from the outset. Its 8ft driving wheels saw it reach speeds that few dared dream about a few years earlier. It covered the 194 miles from Paddington to Exeter in just three hours 28 minutes, at an average speed of 57mph, with Brunel and GWR chairman Charles Russell on board. It took just three minutes longer for the return journey.

It was an unrivalled scientific marvel — turning an uncomfortable jour-ney of several days into a smooth ride of mere hours. Gooch modified the locomotive after he realised that the excess weight over the front carrying wheels was problematic: indeed, the leading axle eventually broke. He extended the frames and turned the locomotive into a 4-2-2.

The Prince class 2-2-2s were the first complete class of locomotives to be built entirely at Swindon. They were effectively stopgaps while Gooch came up with another masterpiece of locomotive design for the

Paddington-Exeter runs in the form of the 29-strong class of Iron Duke 2-2-2s, all with 8ft driving wheels.

The name of that illustrious class was derived from the fact that the trial run of the first took place on April 29, 1847, the Duke of Wellington's birthday. That first locomotive was called *Iron Duke* and it gave its name to the type. Swindon built 22 more, while the other seven on order were farmed out to Rothwell & Co at Bolton.

Again, they produced world-beating speeds. In 1848, *Great Britain* ran between Paddington and Didcot at an average of 67mph. The class allowed regular 60mph trains to be timetabled — not bad at all even by modern day standards. *Lord of the Isles* became a star exhibit at the Great Exhibition of 1851. *Iron Duke* itself ran 607,412 miles before it was withdrawn in August 1873. Three Iron Dukes, *Great Britain, Prometheus* and *Estaffete*, were extensively rebuilt as 4-2-2s with new frames and boilers between May and July 1870, keeping their original names.

Afterwards, more Iron Dukes (known as the Alma class after 1865) were built to similar specifications between August 1871 and July 1888. Known as the Rover class, they were not rebuilds like the first three, but new locomotives, carrying the names of the ones they replaced. Some of them may have included parts from their predecessors. By 1848, the floorspace of Swindon Works had doubled. More than 2000 men were employed by 1851, when a new locomotive was emerging from the erecting shop each week.

Between 1846 and 1858, 39 passenger and 109 goods locomotives were built for the GWR broad gauge network... and 24 engines to 4ft 8½in gauge for other companies, the first in 1855. The Pyracmon class six of 0-6-0 freight locomotives, slightly bigger than the Premiers, appeared in 1847. They were followed by the eight-strong Caesar class of freight 0-6-0s, which emerged in 1851.

The first tank engines, as opposed to tender locomotives, constructed at Swindon were a pair of 4-4-0 saddle tanks for passenger trains in 1849.

However, the biggest class of all was Gooch's Standard Goods, or Ariadne class, of which 102 were built at Swindon between 1852-63, and they were so effective that examples survived in service until 1892.

The opening and overnight success of the Liverpool & Manchester Railway in 1830, pictured running through Olive Mount Cutting, was a big wake-up call to the merchants of Bristol, who saw the great rival port as taking yet more of their trade away because they had a railway.

Goldsworthy Gurney was the first inventor to run steam between London and Bristol, but by road, not rail. Here is his steam carriage of 1829.

The coat of arms of the Great Western Railway, comprising a joining of those of the cities of London and Bristol.
SANDY JJ GOULD*

RIGHT: Brunel's 7ft 0¼in broad gauge, as recreated in a modern-day replica running line at Didcot Railway Centre. The middle rail has been laid to facilitate standard gauge running on broad gauge track, making it mixed gauge.
ROBIN JONES

George Jones, John Harford, Thomas Richard Guppy and William Tothill, the four founders of what became the Great Western Railway, held their first meeting in an office in Temple Back, a street in Bristol which later became redeveloped as the company's goods yard at Temple Meads.

The GWR's original basic terminus at Paddington, then a rural village.

Cattle graze idyllically beneath the recently built Wharncliffe Viaduct at the dawn of the GWR. The Grade I listed brick-built Wharncliffe Viaduct between Southall and Hanwell stations was built in 1836-1837 and was the first major structural design by Isambard Kingdom Brunel, the first building contract to be let on the GWR project and the first major engineering work to be completed. It was also the first railway viaduct to be built with hollow piers, which are now home to a colony of bats.

A typical GWR Brunel broad gauge signal. ROBIN JONES

The 68p Royal Mail stamp produced in 2006 to mark the bicentenary of Isambard Kingdom Brunel's birth shows a broad gauge train crossing Maidenhead bridge. Almost two centuries after critics said that the bridge would soon fall down, it is still standing firm. ROBIN JONES

Navvies completing the building of the great Sonning Cutting, as drawn by J C Bourne.

When the line between Reading and Steventon opened on June 1, 1840, Pangbourne was the first station out of Reading.

Swindon station and sidings as built.

Building the great incline at Wootton Bassett. The distinctive broad gauge track can be seen in detail.

The Three Arches at Chippenham viewed from the west, as sketched by J C Bourne.

The exterior of Brunel's Old Station today. It is built almost at right angles to the later Temple Meads station. ROBIN JONES

The interior of Brunel's original station at Temple Meads.

Fox's Wood tunnel entrance, showing the castellated portal, as portrayed by J C Bourne.

Brunel's bridge over the Avon immediately to the west of Bath station was constructed in timber, but replaced with a steel version in the 1890s.

J C Bourne's view of the interior of Bath station, the frontage of which was designed to complement the city's Regency buildings.

The construction of the 'artistic' cutting through Bath's Sydney Gardens.

A broad gauge locomotive emerges from Box Tunnel's classic western portal. This coloured sketch based on a work by J C Bourne remains one of the distinctive images of Brunel's broad gauge system.

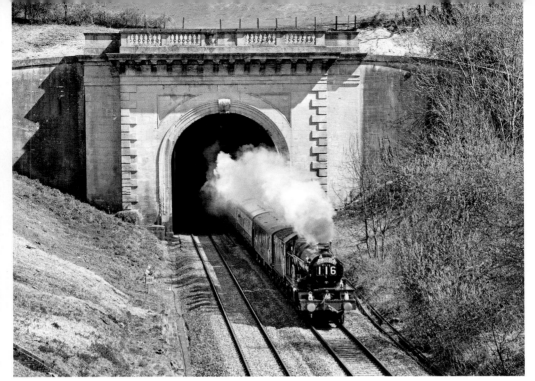

GWR 4-6-0 No. 5043 *Earl of Mount Edgcumbe* storms out of Box Tunnel with Vintage Trains' 'The Bristolian' on April 17, 2010. Restored from Barry scrapyard condition at Tyseley Locomotive Works in Birmingham, it managed the Bristol Temple Meads-Paddington trip in just under 110 minutes start to stop, at an average speed of 64.2mph – just five minutes under the GWR and British Railways timing. BOB GREEN

J C Bourne's depiction of the gloomy interior of the tunnel.

RIGHT: The tunnel through which supplies were brought into the bunker city by rail.
M HESKETH-ROBERTS/ENGLISH HERITAGE

An early 20th century postcard view of the less-celebrated eastern portal of Box Tunnel. To the right is the branch which led into the underground Bath stone quarries, which later became a Second World War ammunition depot and a colossal bunker city during the Cold War. The tunnel which allowed the freight spur into the bunker city has now been bricked up.

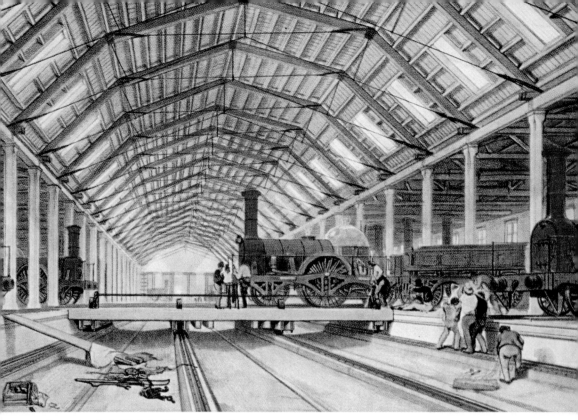

The engine shed at Swindon Works in its early years.

The first locomotive built in its entirety at Swindon works was 2-2-2 *Great Western*.

Daniel Gooch, the locomotive superintendent appointed to the GWR by Isambard Brunel, with a miniature version of a Firefly locomotive.

This watercolour by Sean Bolan depicts one of Daniel Gooch's Iron Duke locomotives at Chippenham station around 1850. NRM

Clear road ahead: there was no cab or weather protection on the early broad gauge locomotives, and the drivers and firemen achieved record-breaking speeds while exposed to the elements.

A broad gauge train near Bathampton, possibly the 3pm service from Bristol to Paddington. GREAT WESTERN TRUST

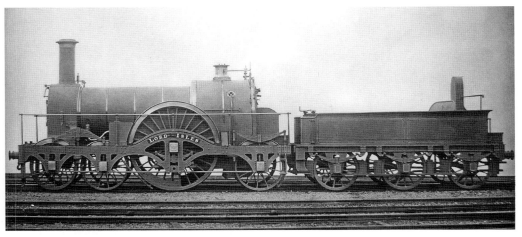

The legendary Iron Duke class locomotive *Lord of the Isles*.

North Star was supplied by Robert Stephenson & Co. It was preserved after withdrawal in 1871 but cut up in 1906. Many components were salvaged, however, and formed the basis of this Swindon-built replica. It is now on display inside STEAM – Museum of the Great Western Railway at Swindon, although it has never been able to move on its own. ROBIN JONES

Although there has been no 7ft 0¼in broad gauge passenger-carrying route in Britain for well over a century, we are able to savour the spectacle of a full-size Gooch Firefly 2-2-2 in action at Didcot Railway Centre. This is a replica of *Fire Fly*, which ran under its own power for the first time at Didcot on March 2, 2005. FRANK DUMBLETON

Broad gauge transport: the first third class passengers on the GWR sat in open wagons, and such was the novelty of travelling at speed, were probably either delighted to do so or scared out of their wits! FRANK DUMBLETON

In 1985 a working replica of *Iron Duke* using parts from two Hunslet Austerity 0-6-0 saddle tanks with a matching open carriage was constructed as part of the Great Western 150 celebrations. It was built to resemble Gooch's 1847 drawings, complete with the exposed wooden lagging of the pre-1848 examples. It is pictured during a visit to Toddington station on the Gloucestershire Warwickshire Railway in 2010. ROBIN JONES

A contemporary engraving of the SS *Great Western*.

John Walter's contemporary engraving of the SS *Great Britain* being floated for the first time, on July 19, 1843, as all Bristol celebrated.

A major tourist attraction in the 21st century: SS *Great Britain* in its dry dock alongside Bristol's Floating Harbour. DAVID NOTON

Rain, Steam and Speed – The Great Western Railway by J M W Turner was first exhibited at the Royal Academy in 1844, though it may have been painted earlier. Who knows – could Jim Hurst have been driving the train, believed to be crossing Maidenhead Bridge, which was designed by Brunel and completed in 1838? The painting is now in the collection of the National Gallery in London.

Jim Hurst, who became the first Great Western Railway locomotive driver. GWR

An artist's impression of the interior of an early royal saloon carrying Victoria, Albert and her family.

Queen Victoria's first journey on the GWR on June 13, 1842, as recreated on its 170th anniversary at Didcot Railway Centre, complete with the modern-day replica broad gauge 2-2-2 *Fire Fly*, standing in for *Phlegethon* with volunteer Beth Gillham taking the role of the monarch.

The 14 Bristol & Exeter Railway broad gauge 4-2-4Ts were built to three different designs, the first entering service in 1853 and the last being withdrawn by the GWR in 1885. The designs featured single large flangeless driving wheels and two supporting bogies. The water was carried in both well and back tanks, leaving the boilers exposed in the same way as tender locomotives. This is No. 40, which was in service from 1853-73. TONY HISGETT*

A truly atmospheric railway: the pumping station at Dawlish in a painting by Condy, with the vacuum pipe running between the rails. ELTON COLLECTION, IRONBRIDGE GORGE MUSEUM TRUST

A section of atmospheric railway vacuum pipe on display at Didcot Railway Centre. It survived because it was used for decades as a stormwater outlet at Goodrington beach near Paignton. ROBIN JONES

A Rover broad gauge 4-2-2 heads a train out of Teignmouth, years after the atmospheric system had been abandoned.

The new Paddington station as seen on July 8, 1854.

Brunel's original Paddington train shed was enlarged by the building of a fourth span in 1916. NETWORK RAIL

An aerial view of Paddington station as seen in October 2010. NETWORK RAIL

The giant tubular girder that formed the Devon side of the Royal Albert Bridge at Saltash is lifted into place.

This view of the Royal Albert Bridge at Saltash by Colin Grace was the runner-up to the Network Rail Lines in the Landscape special award in the Take a View Landscape Photographer of the Year 2010. The bridge has been strengthened several times since it was built, and in 1964, a second Tamar crossing was opened alongside Brunel's. NETWORK RAIL

The timber trestle Moorswater Viaduct was the biggest of all Brunel's viaducts in Cornwall.

End of the line from Paddington: Penzance station as depicted on a hand-coloured postcard of 1908.

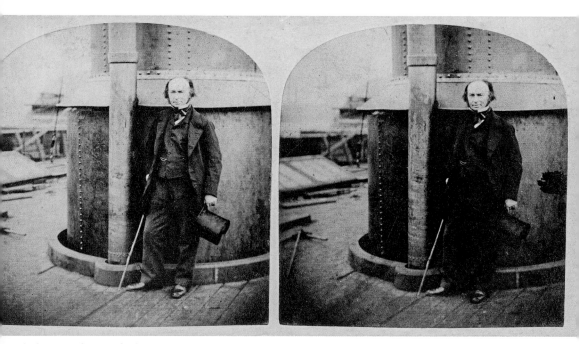

The last-ever photograph of Isambard Kingdom Brunel was finally published in 2019, 160 years after his death. The rare stereoscopic photograph shows a man almost unrecognisable from his iconic, ruthless image. Brunel stands on board the SS *Great Eastern*, his third and final ship, leaning heavily on his walking stick for support. There is a slight puffiness to his face and fingers, and he already looks like a sick man. Towards midday on the occasion, he suffered a fit of paralysis – some say a heart attack – and was taken back to his home in Duke Street. SS GREAT BRITAIN TRUST

The last broad gauge 'Cornishman' left Paddington at 10.15am on May 20, 1892, hauled by *Great Western*.

Marking the 120th anniversary of the gauge conversion, Great Western Society volunteers re-enacted the part of the tracklayers of 1892. Here is the gang packing ballast under the baulk beneath the broad gauge running line at Didcot Railway Centre in May 2012. FRANK DUMBLETON

Broad gauge track being converted to standard gauge at Millbay.

Nowhere left to go: rows and rows of perfectly serviceable broad gauge engines await the cutter's torch at Swindon in 1892 because there is no longer any track on which to run them.

An armada of hot air balloons floats over Clifton Suspension Bridge during the Bristol Balloon Fiesta.
GARY NEWMAN/VISIT BRISTOL

The broad gauge carriage replica inside the Being Brunel museum in Bristol. BEING BRUNEL

Magnificent Clevedon Pier was built from second-hand rails that were supplied for use on one of Brunel's broad gauge railways and opened in 1869. ROBIN JONES

City of Truro, which unofficially became the first steam locomotive to break the 100mph barrier in 1904, at Cheltenham Racecourse station on the Gloucestershire Warwickshire Railway in 2009. In February 2013, the National Railway Museum permanently retired it from service after a boiler tube leak was discovered. ROBIN JONES

Evening Star on display in the Great Hall of the National Railway Museum at York. ROBIN JONES

Preserved Western Region Class 52 diesel hydraulic D1015 *Western Champion* pilots BR Britannia Pacific No. 70013 *Oliver Cromwell* away from Bodmin Parkway (formerly Bodmin Road) in July 2007 over what was a section of the Cornwall Railway. BRIAN SHARPE

Two eras side by side at Paddington: GWR 4-6-0 No. 5043 *Earl of Mount Edgcumbe*, heading the 'Great Britain IV' tour in April 2012, next to a First Great Western Class 125 High Speed Train. BRIAN SHARPE

In 1860, the GWR ordered a rolling mill to be built at Swindon to repair damaged rails. It attracted huge numbers of workers from South Wales, creating a large Welsh community.

By the middle of the 1860s, demand for new railway rolling stock was soaring as Britain underwent a trade boom, and Swindon's order book was so full that it had to turn work away. The GWR established extra workshops at Wolverhampton, Worcester and Saltney in Cheshire to cope. In 1868, Swindon also became the central workshop for the construction of GWR carriages and wagons. A new carriage and wagon works was built to the north of Swindon station, complete with 13 miles of sidings. Swindon's boiler and tender making workshops were opened in 1875.

While the town rapidly expanded along with the works, and the GWR went from strength to strength as its empire expanded, there was no let-up in the care which the company showed to its workers and their families who lived near its workshops.

A GWR Medical Fund Society financed a cottage hospital in Swindon. Workers paid a weekly subscription to a complete medical service, including doctors' surgeries, dental and eye clinics, subsidised by the GWR.

It was the first of its kind in the world. It has been claimed that Aneurin Bevan used it as the blueprint for Britain's National Health Service a century later.

CHAPTER EIGHT

Next stop: New York Central!

L ADIES AND gentlemen: the HS5 service from Glasgow Alex Ferguson terminus will be departing in five minutes. We will be arriving at London Thames Estuary Skyport at 10.30am, for onward connections via Virgin Orbital sub-space transporter for Beijing to arrive approximately 90 minutes later...

Such a scenario seems laughable today, but then the idea of travelling from London to Bristol in four hours rather than four days would have seemed equally far-fetched in the late 18th century. And the prospect of adding North America as a final and achievable destination for ordinary members of the public would have seemed like utter nonsense.

Since the days of Cabot, Bristol had found itself perfectly poised as a launch pad for exploiting the potential of North America. However, that was primarily for trade — although there was a growing number of émigrés seeking a new life in the New World. Brunel was well aware of Bristol's link to America and it formed an integral part of his grand vision. It was not only in the field of railways, bridges and tunnels that he thought big.

Whereas his contemporaries would have been more than content with overseeing the construction of a new and revolutionary railway from London to Bristol, Isambard the dazzling young engineer extraordinaire — and workaholic — was in parallel enacting plans to create the world's first transatlantic liners.

Shipping was the last major area to benefit from the massive strides in transport technology spawned by the Industrial Revolution. During the 1830s it still owed more to traditional building techniques than the application of modern science — but that would end with Brunel.

Water transport had been far slower than railways to take up the concept of steam power, although Scot William Symington had fitted a James Watt stationary steam engine inside a boat which was trialled on a loch at Dalswinton near Dumfries on October 14, 1788, reputedly with the poet Robert Burns on board. This was years before Richard Trevithick's first public demonstration of a steam railway locomotive.

In 1812 Henry Bell's *Comet* on the River Clyde became the first steam-operated commercial ferry. Two years later, none other than Marc Brunel launched the steamboat *Regent*, which ran between London and Margate. His son was clearly inspired, as events more than two decades later would show.

The first cross-channel steamship was the 112-ton *Hibernia* which made the trip from Holyhead to Dublin in seven hours in 1816. The first oceanic crossing by a steamship was made in 1819 by the SS *Savannah*, built by Francis Fickett, of Corlears Hook, New York, which reached Liverpool from Savannah, Georgia, in 29 days 11 hours, but mostly using its sails.

Early steamships were considered suitable only for short runs in comparatively shallow waters, because they lacked the capacity to carry and burn sufficient coal for a transatlantic voyage. Bigger ships meant bigger loads of coal, increasing the weight and the demand for power, the logic of the day dictated, and even Marc Brunel subscribed to that belief.

Isambard disagreed. He saw that the energy needed to drive any ship, whether by sail or steam, depended on the weight of the water that it has to shift, not on the weight of the vessel itself. He discovered that the larger the ship, the better the crucial energy-to-weight equation.

It is said that at an October 1835 meeting of the GWR directors at Ridley's Hotel in Blackfriars, London, Isambard came up with the idea of extending the projected railway by adding a steamship service from

Bristol to New York. His 'super ship' was to have the ideal name — *Great Western*.

He was backed by board member Thomas Guppy, who convinced the other three to examine the possibility. The GWR enlisted the help of naval captain Christopher Claxton, an acquaintance of Brunel who had access to official drawings of Admiralty ships under construction.

The first meeting of the new Great Western Steamship Company took place on March 3, 1836. It aimed to build two ships, each costing £25,000. Five of the board members were also GWR directors.

Made of oak, the ship was to be the first steamship purposely built for the Atlantic crossing. It was an iron-strapped wooden side-wheel paddle steamer and equipped with auxiliary sails. Brunel's idea was for it to replace sail power on the regularly scheduled transatlantic packet boat services which had been operating under sail since 1818.

The keel of this first ship was laid in June 1836 in shipbuilder William Patterson's yard at Wapping in the Floating Harbour. At 205ft, it was the longest ever to have been laid, and on August 28, crowds flocked to see the stern post raised and the stern frame positioned.

All told, the vessel totalled 236ft in length and displaced 2300 tonnes of water, Brunel taking on board the stresses which would be placed on it by the Atlantic surges. The ship was of conventional structural design with oak frames forming the bottom and sides, so for extra strength he added four staggered rows of iron bolts running the entire length of the ship.

The hull was sheathed in copper below the waterline. Lambeth manufacturer Maudslay, Son & Field, which had worked for Marc Brunel, was contracted to supply a pair of steam engines for the ship. These engines, which had cylinders with a massive 73½in diameter and a stroke of 7ft, were to drive twin paddle wheels 28ft in diameter.

Although the huge boilers took up almost half its interior, the ship was designed to carry 148 passengers, with a main passenger saloon 75ft long by 34ft at its widest.

Finally, on July 19, 1837, more than 50,000 spectators turned out both on the docksides and on other ships in the harbour to watch the SS *Great Western* launched. It was named by Mrs Miles, the wife of one of the steamship company's directors, as Claxton cracked a bottle of Madeira over the bowsprit.

Finally, the ship was towed down the muddy Avon estuary by the steam tug *Lion* and, accompanied by the steam packet *Benledi*, using a four-masted Maudslay spent six months fitting much of the machinery in Blackwall's East India Dock.

March 1838 saw *Great Western* moved to a berth in the River Thames for preliminary trials to take place. However, it struck another ship as it tried to avoid a barge, and days later it became marooned on a mudbank opposite Trinity Wharf. Amends were, however, more than made when during four days of engine trials it managed an average speed of 11 knots comfortably. The critics — and there were many — who said the SS *Great Western* would never work were proved wrong again.

TRANSATLANTIC STEAMSHIP RACE

On March 31, 1838, the SS *Great Western* sailed for Avonmouth to begin its maiden voyage to New York. However, prior to reaching Avonmouth, a fire broke out in the engine room. During the panic that erupted, Brunel fell 20ft and was injured, having to then go ashore at Canvey Island for treatment.

The fire was contained and caused little damage, but in the days when passengers were scared to ride through railway tunnels, more than 50 cancelled their bookings to New York.

When the SS *Great Western* finally departed Avonmouth, there were just seven passengers on board. There was an added impetus for this first trip though; rivals the British and American Steam Navigation Company wanted to run the first steam-powered regularly scheduled transatlantic packet service with its SS *British Queen*. However, it became clear that the ship would not be ready in time and that the SS *Great Western* would beat them.

So the British and American Steam Navigation Company hired the *Sirius*, a cross-channel steamship. It set out from Ireland on April 4 — four days before the SS *Great Western* departed from Bristol, having been delayed by the fire.

The *Sirius* reached New York first, but only by a day. It also carried 40 passengers, but such was the panic to get there ahead of the rival ship, the crew burned the cabin furniture, spare yards and one mast, in order to raise sufficient steam, its coal having almost run out.

When Brunel's ship arrived, after just 15 days at sea, not 18, it still had 200 tons of coal aboard.

The Americans were delighted by the race between the two ships. So many people wanted to board the SS *Great Western* that the captain was forced to issue tickets in order to restrict the numbers.

Going back, Brunel's ship reached Britain in 14 days as compared to the 18 taken by her rival. And that was all before the opening of the first section of the Great Western Railway on June 4, 1838.

SS *Great Western* proved an immediate commercial success, making 67 crossings in eight years. During 1838-40, she averaged 16 days, 0 hours (7.95 knots) outwards to New York and 13 days, 9 hours (9.55 knots) home.

The SS *Great Western* influenced the design of other Atlantic paddle steamers. Cunard's *Britannia* was a scaled-down version of SS *Great Western*. However, the SS *Great Western* could not fit through the lock gates leading into the Floating Harbour, and accrued high mooring charges by having to be moored in King's Road in the Bristol Channel. When it left Bristol for New York on February 11, 1843, it was the last departure of a transatlantic liner from the port for 28 years. Bristol's importance as a port for Atlantic trade went into decline, and all because the harbour authorities refused to widen the lock gates to accommodate new bigger ships.

Taken out of service at Liverpool in 1846, the SS *Great Western* was sold to the Royal Mail Steam Packet Company and used on voyages to the Gulf of Mexico for a decade. It was acquired by the Government in 1856 and ended its days as a troopship during the Crimean War before being scrapped on the lower reaches of the Thames at Castle's salvage yard in 1857.

MAKE WAY FOR THE GREAT IRON SHIP

In many ways, the SS *Great Western* was a halfway house between sail and steam technology, and in 1838, not content to dwell on its international success, Brunel and the steamship company began looking at ways to better its design for their second ship.

Steam power was obviously the way forward. At first, Brunel, Guppy and Claxton looked at a 254ft-long oak ship with even bigger paddle wheels, until they saw John Laird's 213ft English Channel packet ship *Rainbow* — the biggest iron-hulled ship then in service — arrive in Bristol.

The sight gripped Isambard's imagination and a detailed examination was made of the vessel. Brunel sent Claxton and Patterson on a return voyage to Antwerp to assess iron-hull technology and both returned singing its praise. Accordingly, Brunel scrapped his plans to build an oak sister ship and persuaded the company directors to go for an iron-hulled one instead.

Iron-hulled ships were by then nothing new: the first had appeared in 1787 in the form of a 70ft-long canal barge aptly built by John 'Iron Mad' Wilkinson, a partner in the successful project to build the world's first iron bridge, over the Severn Gorge. The first iron steamship, the *Aaron Derby*, appeared in 1821. Iron-hulled ships were 30% lighter than wooden vessels and their thinner sides provided more hull space.

Furthermore, at the time, wood was becoming more expensive in Britain, while iron was getting cheaper. Iron hulls did not suffer from woodworm or dry rot, and had a much greater structural strength, allowing longer ships to be built.

Between September 1838 and June 1839, six different designs were produced. The one chosen was Brunel's box girder-type hull with a two-skinned cellular construction. It had six water-tight compartments and two longitudinal bulkheads, plus a strong iron deck.

Brunel's design team was learning on the job. Still thinking about the design of wooden ships, they cautiously gave more and more ground to the iron hull principles, and the ship grew bigger and bigger with each new blueprint.

Eventually, the design featured a ship with a capacity of 3400 tons, more than 1000 tons larger than any ship then in existence. Nicknamed the 'Mammoth', the keel for the new ship was laid in Patterson's yard on July 19, 1839.

Just as with the *Rainbow*, Isambard was enthralled by the sight of the world's first screw propeller-driven steamship, Francis Pettit Smith's *Archimedes*, which entered the Floating Harbour in May 1840, just a few months after being completed by the Propeller Steamship Company.

Guppy took a trip aboard her to Liverpool, and his report impressed the steamship company so much that it called a halt to all work on the paddle steamers for its second ship. Instead, the *Archimedes* was booked for six months of tests in order to find the most efficient design of propeller. Finally, a new four-bladed design by Smith was selected.

Brunel then took the bold step of asking the Great Western Steamship Company to change direction, scrapping the original paddle wheel engines which were half built, and designing new ones to turn a screw propeller.

He outlined the advantages of screw propulsion. The machinery was lighter and improved fuel economy, while it could be positioned lower in the hull, reducing the ship's centre of gravity and making it more stable in heavy seas, and at the same time took up less room, freeing more space for cargo.

Getting rid of cumbersome paddle boxes would decrease resistance through the water, and while depth of a paddlewheel is constantly changing, depending on the ship's cargo and the movement of waves, a propeller remains fully submerged and at full efficiency at all times. Screw propulsion equipment was also cheaper. Brunel won the directors over yet again, but the change of design led to a substantial delay for the completion of the ship.

The U-turn delivered nothing less than a fatal blow to ambitious young engineer Francis Humphrys, who had been picked against Isambard's advice by the directors above Maudslay to build what would have been the world's biggest marine engine for the ship as originally planned. After being ordered to redesign the paddle engines which were already at an advanced stage, he resigned and died of a 'brain fever' a few days later.

Isambard then took over the design of the 1600hp engines himself, and based it on the Triangle type patented by Marc Brunel.

The steamship company leased land next to the Floating Harbour and turned the site into the world's first integrated steamship works, building the engines inside. The iron plates for the outside of the hull were made at Horsehay Ironworks in Coalbrookdale and brought to Bristol by canal.

In July 1839, workmen in a specially built dock in Bristol harbour started to bend, shape, hammer and rivet the hull of what was to become the SS *Great Britain*. It had been hoped to have the ship built by 1841, but it was not to be. The cost of the project soared, and ended up at £125,555, double that of the SS *Great Western*. However, by then Brunel's big railway had been such a success that investors had little hesitation in backing his scheme.

The SS *Great Britain* was launched on July 19, 1843, exactly six years after the *SS Great Western*. The GWR brought Prince Albert from London on a special train driven by Daniel Gooch himself. The Royal Consort took his place as guest of honour after being greeted by the Lord Mayor of Bristol at Temple Meads station.

Marc and Sophia Brunel watched with pride as the dry dock was flooded to allow their son's giant ship to float. Mrs Miles was again brought forward to name the ship, but the bottle of champagne missed its target. Albert stepped forward to complete the job and smashed a second bottle on the bows, naming the ship the SS *Great Britain*, which was described as "the greatest experiment since the creation".

Immediately afterwards, the ship was moved back into the dry dock to be fitted out. It was ready in March 1844, but then it was discovered that it was too big to pass through the locks linking the Floating Harbour to the Avon.

Isambard was the dock company's consulting engineer. He persuaded its directors to approve modifications allowing the SS *Great Britain* to pass the Junction Lock into Cumberland Basin, which it did on October 26, 1844, after a delicate day-long operation.

Trials were undertaken in the Bristol Channel on December 12, January 10 and January 20 before the ship went on a 40-hour voyage to London three days later, averaging 12½ knots despite bad weather.

With SS *Great Britain* moored on the Thames for five months, Queen Victoria and Prince Albert had a guided tour on April 22. The vessel was bigger than any ship previously built, 322ft long and having a 3400-ton displacement. It had four decks, required a crew of 120, and was fitted to accommodate 360 passengers plus with 1200 tons of cargo and a similar tonnage of coal for fuel.

Two giant propeller engines with a combined weight of 340 tons and each capable of developing 1000hp were built to a modified patent of Marc Brunel. The steam was provided by three 34ft saltwater boilers, each having eight furnaces. The ship was also provided with secondary sail power, in the form of one square-rigged and five schooner-rigged iron masts. The interior was divided into three decks, the upper two of which were used for passenger accommodation and the lower for cargo.

FLAGSHIP OF AN EMPIRE

At the time the SS *Great Britain* was set to make its first Atlantic crossing, the British Empire was nearing its zenith, and the ship was viewed by many as a pinnacle of achievement — showing the world just what the nation was capable of achieving.

Its maiden transatlantic trip was from Liverpool on July 26, when the Great Western Railway had been running just over four years. The SS *Great Britain* carried only 45 passengers and arrived in New York just 15 days later at an average speed of more than nine knots. Yet on its second trip to North America the ship sustained several incidents of propeller damage. It was forced to return to Liverpool under sail power alone, but still made the journey in only 20 days.

A third voyage was made to New York on May 29, 1846. On the homeward journey, the SS *Great Britain* made the crossing in just 13 days at an average speed of 13 knots. For the Victorians, this was the equivalent of our space age technology.

Disaster struck on the fifth trip when the ship ran aground in Dundrum Bay, Ireland, on September 22, with 180 passengers on board. Captain Hosken declared that his instruments had been affected by the iron hull and he believed that he was off the coast of the Isle of Man. There were no casualties.

The ship was holed in two places, but the sheer strength of its structure prevented it from breaking up. Claxton built two breakwaters around the beached ship to protect it, but in vain. The owners were running out of money and Isambard finally went out to Ireland to supervise the salvage mission himself. Raging that the ship had been left "like a useless saucepan", he ordered a protective barrier of 5000 faggots to be piled against the side of the ship that faced the sea.

Eventually, on August 27, 1847, the steamship was towed off the beach by HMS *Birkenhead*. The Great Western Steamship Company could not afford the £22,000 repairs in addition to the £12,670 towing charge and it was decided to sell off all of the ship's fixtures and fittings. They then sold the vessel itself to Liverpool shipping firm Bright, Gibbs & Co, former agent of the Great Western Steamship Company, for a bargain £18,000.

When the steamship company was wound up in February 1852, Patterson bought the lease on its dockyard. The new owner refitted the ship, including the installation of new engines, and the SS *Great Britain* was back in service in May 1852, when she made her comeback voyage to Melbourne, Australia, carrying 630 emigrants. Such was the interest in the ship down under that 4000 spectators paid a shilling each to inspect it.

It spent 24 years working the route to Australia, barring brief spells as a troopship during the Crimean War, and during the Indian Mutiny, before being sold to Antony Gibbs, Sons & Co in 1876 for use as a transatlantic cargo sailing ship, losing its engines during the conversion.

DEATH AND REBIRTH

The steamless ship had problems round Cape Horn in April 1886, losing two masts and sustaining several severe leaks. Shelter was sought at Port Stanley in the Falkland Isles, where it was found that it would cost too much to repair. The once proud ship was again sold off, this time to the Falkland Islands Company as a store ship for coal and wood.

The ship was towed out of the harbour in 1937 and beached at Sparrow Cove, with holes knocked in its stern to ensure that it would never float again. During the Second World War, some of its iron was scavenged to repair HMS *Exeter*, one of the Royal Navy ships that fought the German 'pocket battleship' the *Admiral Graf Spee* and was badly damaged during the Battle of the River Plate.

However, there were many who never forgot the ship that was once the pride of an empire, and the envy of the rest of the world. A naval architect visited the islands in 1968 and established that it was possible to refloat the SS *Great Britain*, with the aid of a pontoon submerged beneath its hull. With the pontoon pumped out, the ship lifted on top of it.

On top of the pontoon, and beginning on April 24, 1970, the SS *Great Britain* made one last voyage, all 7000 miles back to Bristol, towed by the salvage tug *Varuis II*. The journey went via Montevideo and lasted until June 22, when Bristol tugs hauled the pontoon into the docks at Avonmouth. There, the SS *Great Britain* was lifted off the pontoon in the graving dock and refloated in its own right.

On July 5, the sides of the Avon estuary were packed as the ship was towed upstream to Y Wharf in Bristol's docks. The salvage team had to wait a fortnight for a spring tide high enough to allow the hulk to be eased into the Great Western dry dock off the Floating Harbour on July 19, 127 years to the day that it was launched in 1843.

It took another 35 years to complete the full restoration of the ship, which is now permanently moored in its dry dock off the Floating Harbour, and is not only a major award-winning international tourist attraction listed as part of the National Historic Fleet Core Collection and attracting between 150,000–170,000 visitors each year, but also a defining symbol of Bristol in its finest hour.

In 1998, an extensive survey discovered that the hull was continuing to corrode in the humid atmosphere of the dock. It was said that the ship would have just 20 years left before it rusted away to the point of no return.

Extensive conservation work then commenced, centred around the pioneering installation of a 'glass sea' at the waterline of the restored ship to act as a giant airtight chamber, protecting its lower hull. Beneath the glass plate, moisture is removed from the air using special dehumidification equipment, keeping the space beneath at 22% relative humidity and preventing further corrosion. The glass surface is covered with a thin layer of water, so the ship appears to visitors to be floating.

SIX TIMES BIGGER THAN SS *GREAT BRITAIN*

Brunel had succeeded in linking London to New York via two Great Westerns, or one GWR and one SS *Great Britain*. His next steamship project was to be his last — the SS *Great Eastern*.

The Eastern Steamship Company was created to build a ship which was six times bigger than the *Great Britain*. It needed to be, since it was intended for use on long voyages to the Far East, where there were no coal bunkering facilities, and so sufficient supplies had to be taken on board. It would be powered by both propellers and paddle wheels.

Contracts were awarded in 1853; James Watt and Co was to build the propeller engines and John Scott Russell was the main contractor, responsible for building the paddle engines and the ship itself. The keel was laid down in February 1854 at Millwall on the Isle of Dogs. Despite Russell going bankrupt in early 1856, the ship was ready for launch at the end of October 1857. It was so big that it had to be launched sideways, a new technique devised by Brunel.

Miss Hope, daughter of one of the directors, broke a bottle of champagne on the ship on November 7, 1857, naming it *Leviathan*. Tragically, it did not slide into the water as planned. The brake handle of a chain for controlling the slide flew up, killing one workman and injuring four others. The ship then refused to budge another inch.

It took nearly three months to inch it towards the water, but on January 30, 1858, it floated at last, by which time the cost of building it had doubled to £732,000 and the Eastern Steamship Company went into liquidation. The vessel was towed to Deptford and was laid up for a year before being was acquired by a new owner, the Great Ship Company, and finished in August 1859 under the name of the SS *Great Eastern*. It weighed 18,915 tons gross, with 27,859 tonnes displacement — a tonnage record that remained intact until the launching of the liner *Lusitania* in 1907.

The SS *Great Eastern's* combination of paddle and propeller engines provided great manoeuvrability. It was the first of the famous luxury ocean liners, with berths for 4000 passengers, first class cabins which offered hot and cold running water for baths and a gas plant which illuminated five saloons.

However, the SS *Great Eastern* is another story, for while it further exemplified the genius of Brunel, it has little to do with the story of his big railway, which before it reached its initial goals of Bristol and via steamship to New York, was already striking out for new destinations...

CHAPTER NINE

The first Great Western Railway driver

T HE FIRST locomotive driver appointed to the Great Western Railway was Jim Hurst, an illiterate native of Lancashire. He became a friend of Daniel Gooch and loved driving at speed. However, he was often fined for misdemeanours and ended up being transferred to Totnes.

He ended his career as a labourer in Swindon Works and retired at the age of 64 to the 'model town' of New Swindon, where he saw out his days in a well-kept company cottage a stone's throw from the great workshops.

His son, also Jim Hurst, started as a Swindon Works apprentice and became its foreman. He went on to become locomotive superintendent of the Jersey Railway. The Great Western Magazine, a regular company publication, once carried an article about Jim — the anonymous writer had visited him to note down his recollections of those seminal years of the GWR and indeed steam railways, beginning with George Stephenson's ground-breaking construction of a railway which 'floated' over the notorious all-consuming peat bog of Chat Moss which had up till then blocked the way from Manchester to Liverpool.

The following are excerpts from the interview.

"Well," the interviewer said, "You know what I have come down for."

"To hear my yarns," said Jim. "Since my wife died suddenly here a few weeks ago, I have thought that my own time won't be long, and that I'd like to leave some account of the few things I know after me."

"Now," said he, "how do you wish me to begin?"

"Begin," the interviewer replied, "from your childhood, and tell the story of your life in your own way, and leave it to me to shape it afterwards."

Without waiting for any further signal, Jim immediately got up steam and started from the platform of his cradle.

"I was born at Astley in Lancashire in the year 1811. My parents were cotton hand loom weavers. I got no schooling. When I was nine years old, I commenced to wind bobbins, and at 10 I went to work a pair of cotton hand looms. Our home was within half a mile of Chat Moss, and I well remember in 1825, when George Stephenson came to have a look at the Moss and see how it would suit for a railway. He wanted some people to show him over the Moss, and he hired my father, another man and myself.

"By George's orders, my father took a large staff to sink into the Moss, while I carried a flint and steel to light a candle, in order that when a sounding was made, George might be able to test whether the air coming from below was coalpit air or not.

"When I saw my father sticking the pole down deep in various parts of the Moss, and the water showing itself and no signs of the coal, I said to George: Us lads had tried that scores of times with sticks, and found the water used to shoot up."

He said: "You lads know better than I do," and then he told me: "I will make a railway man of thee when thee gets old enough." In the year 1826, the Act of Parliament was passed to make the (Liverpool & Manchester) railway, and in that year the work began, and a nice job it was.

"The Moss was like a sponge, and drains had to be constructed. That year my father gave up the weaving and went to work on the line, and he was the first man to put a spade in to make a drain at a place called Burton Moss. My

father afterwards became a small contractor for making the line, employing nine or 10 men, and I joined my father's gang in the year 1827.

"I well remember when the first engine ran over the Moss. George Stephenson used to ride backwards and forwards on it and men who wanted a job gathered in groups along the road. George used to bring them to him in this fashion: he'd stand by the side of the engine and hold up as many fingers as he wanted men.

"When the line opened for traffic in 1830, my father was put in charge of a cattle siding at Salford, and after 23 years in the service of that company was killed on duty. I entered its service the same year as a labourer. The year after, I became a fireman and continued firing for two years and four months. I then became engine driver and held that post till June 1836, when I left the Liverpool & Manchester.

"The foreman of that company's loco works at Salford at the time of my leaving was a kind-hearted old Scotchman, named Sandy Fife; he was a true friend to me. When I parted with him he promised to do his best to get a job for me, and after I was out 13 weeks I got a letter from Sandy that he wanted to see me. He received me very warmly, and said to me: 'Jamie, I've got the choice of four places for you, one in Spain, one in America, one in Germany and one on the Great Western.'

"My mind leaned to the last, on account of it being in England. I learned from Sandy that Mr Gooch, who had often ridden on my engine at the time he was employed at the Vulcan Works, had just been made loco superintendent of the Great Western, and that it was from him the offer of a job on that line came; also that he was about to pass through Salford on his way to London by coach.

"He stopped for a while at Sandy's house, and there I met him. He at once recognised me, gave me a warm greeting and spoke of the old days, and our interview ended in his engaging me as an engine driver for the Great Western at 6s 8d per day. While the engine which I was to drive was getting ready at the Vulcan Works, I worked there as a labourer. That engine was the old Vulcan, *which was many years ago smashed up. In 1837 I left the works and came to London, taking two engines with me, the* Vulcan *and the* Premier. *The latter was built at another shop.*

"They were brought from Liverpool to London by sea, and took six days from port to port. At the London docks, Mr Gooch met me, and by his directions the engines were taken by barge to West Drayton, going up the river and canal, and it was only last year when I was passing Drayton that I saw the old elm still standing which supported the gearing which lifted the engines from the barge. Mr Gooch met me at Drayton, received me very kindly and took me down the village to his own lodgings.

"My first drive on the Great Western was on December 28, 1837. It was a trial trip from the 14th to the 15th milepost close to Langley, and for three-and-a-half months afterwards I daily made short trial trips with Mr Brunel and Mr Gooch. The line opened from Paddington to Taplow on June 4, 1838. On the day of the opening I was placed at Taplow with my engine to act in cases of breakdown, and here I will say a few words about our old engines. I may mention five which were made at the Vulcan Works.

"The Vulcan *and the* Bacchus *had an 8ft wheel, 14in cylinder, and 16in stroke; and, from what I could hear at the time, cost about £1400 each; while the* Apollo, *the* Neptune *and the* Venus *had an 8ft wheel, 12in cylinder, and 16in stroke. The day after the opening, I ran the 8 o'clock morning train from Paddington to Taplow and continued to run that train for about two months. Its usual make-up was nine coaches, and we used to do the journey, after stopping at all stations on the way, in about 1 hour and 40 minutes.*

"Among my most prominent and constant passengers were the officers in Windsor garrison. They used to get out at Slough. Slough station, I may tell you, then consisted of a platform, and the ticket office was in an adjoining beer shop kept by a man named Bragg. The officers of Windsor, who had run up to London the night before, were always most anxious to get to Slough punctually by the 8 o'clock train out, so that they might not be late for parade, and I always did my best to have them to time. They knew this and often gave..."

The interviewer here applied the brakes and told Jim that as his remarks would go into print he should leave the completion of the sentence for the reader's own interpretation, and asked Jim where he lived during the early days of his driving.

"For about the first nine months," said Jim, "I lived at Paddington in a cottage that stood not far from the spot on which the Great Western Hotel has since been built It was a nice little cottage and I had it for six shillings per week.

"From Paddington I went to live at West Drayton, my home there being a cottage made from the materials which were used on Mr Gooch's first Great Western office in that village. From there I went to one of the company's cottages in Taplow Yard, and afterwards I've been to live over a biggish part of the line — Slough, Kemble, Cirencester, Exeter, Newton Abbot, Totnes, Plymouth, Pyle, Swansea, Brimscombe, Newnham, Gloucester, Oxford, Leamington and Swindon."

"How long were you driving for the company?" Jim was asked.

"From 1837 to 1861," he replied. "I then went into the loco works at Swindon and stopped there till 1866, when I had to give up as my health failed me."

"During the time of your driving," the interviewer asked, "I suppose you have had some very narrow escapes?"

"Yes, in 1855, not very far from where the big accident happened at Shipton, some Christmases back, there was an explosion on my engine, I was blown up through the air and my mate was killed; and 13 years before I ran down the bank at Kemble, the accident being caused through a switchman. I had in the train at the time Mr Charles Richardson, the Severn Tunnel engineer."

Jim was asked: "In your time you have often come in contact with Sir Daniel, can you call to mind any little incidents of interest in connection with him?"

"Well," Jim replied, "he was a man who was rather stern and always wanted the work done well, he appreciated a good servant, but a bad one stood no chance with him. He'd have the work done his own way, and plenty of men to do it. If you followed out what he himself told you, you were all right. I heard an officer of the company whose ideas of how things ought to be done were different from Mr Gooch's once said to a brother officer at Reading: 'I don't know how many times I have complained of that Hurst, but it's not the slightest use, Mr Gooch will take no notice of my letters.' 'You might have saved yourself the trouble,' was the answer. 'You may be sure that Hurst has been working according to his superintendent's orders.'

"A man," continued Jim, "cannot serve two masters when they don't agree as how you are to do a thing, can he? Mr Gooch sometimes liked a joke. One

of our earliest drivers was Harry Appleby, a Newcastle man; he was a gruff, surly kind of fellow, and like myself was no scholar. It wasn't my fault I was no scholar, as I told Mr Gooch 47 years ago at Kemble, when he said to me 'Jim, it's a pity you had no schooling.' 'Schooling, sir,' said I, 'at my home was sixpence a week, and my mother could only spare three-ha'-pence. Us old ones had not the chance the young ones have now.'"

Jim related another incident about a fellow employee called Appleby, who he said was of the class of men who would play practical jokes and interfere with other people, but nobody must touch him.

"I remember one day I was driving out of Paddington, Mr Gooch being on my engine; we sighted Appleby, coming in the opposite direction. 'Now Jim,' said Mr Gooch, hiding himself by stooping, 'give Appleby a little steam as he passes.' I obeyed my superintendent's instructions to the best of my ability. In the evening, Appleby met Mr Gooch at Taplow and made a strong complaint against me, and wound up by saying that 'either he or I should go'. He did not know who put me up to use the valve. 'Well, Appleby,' answered Mr Gooch, 'all I can say is this, that the man who gives a joke must be prepared to take one.' This remark closed Appleby up."

The interviewer then asked Jim about old engine drivers and in particular Dick Peacock, who became a great locomotive engineer and partner in an eminent firm of engine builders in Lancashire (Beyer Peacock) and sat in the House of Commons for Gorton Division.

Jim replied: "Oh yes, I remember him well, and the scene at Hay Lane, between Swindon and Wootton Bassett; Peacock came to Swindon about 39 years ago to work for Sheffield & Rotherham, which used to make engines for the company by contract, and Mr Gooch gave him the job of driving one of the engines which that firm made. Well, he had not long started driving when, going to Wootton Bassett, there was a trolley of metals, belonging to the permanent way, on the line. Peacock never noticed it but dashed his engine against it and the engine turned right over on its side. Peacock knew there was no use in going to face Daniel, so he cut like a fox across the fields; and for years we heard no more of him, till he appeared as a big man in Lancashire."

The interviewer commented: "Many engine drivers have made very successful runs on the Great Western, but it strikes me Dick Peacock's most successful run was his run off it."

Jim was justly proud of his own skill as a driver. He became enthusiastic on the subject of breakdowns, and his ingenious methods of rendering 'first aid' to the disabled engine. Describing one such incident, he said: "My engine limped along and Mr Brunel, who was on her, turned to me and said: 'You may as well give up Hurst, you'll never get her to Paddington.' 'Leave it to me,' said I, 'I will'... and I did."

CHAPTER TEN

The first royal train

IT WAS Brunel's big railway which had the honour of running Britain's first royal train. On June 13, 1842, Queen Victoria became the first British monarch to journey by train, travelling between Slough, the nearest station for Windsor Castle where she had been staying, and Paddington, accompanied by Prince Albert.

The Times carried a detailed report of the event as follows:

The intention of Her Majesty to return to town by railroad was first intimated to the authorities at Paddington on Saturday afternoon, and, in consequence, preparations on an extensive scale were ordered to be made for the transit of the royal pair from Slough to the Paddington terminus, which were carried into effect with the greatest secrecy.

Immediately after the departure of the day mail train from Paddington at a quarter past 10 o'clock, the royal train, consisting of the Phlegethon *engine and tender, drawing the royal saloon in the centre of two royal saloon carriages, preceded by a second-class carriage and followed by three carriage-trucks, started from the terminus at Paddington for Slough, which station they reached shortly before 11 o'clock.*

Previously to the departure from Paddington, the royal saloon, the fittings of which are upon a most elegant and magnificent scale, were tastefully improved by bouquets of rare flowers arranged within the carriage.

At Slough, the royal party on their arrival at the station, a few minutes before 12 o'clock in six carriages, were received by Mr O Russell (the chairman), Mr F P Barlow, one of the directors, and Mr C Saunders, the secretary of the railway company, and conducted to the splendid apartments at the station designed for the reception of Royalty. Her Majesty, however, during the delay necessarily occasioned by the placing the carriages of the attendants on the tracks, proceeded to the line, and examined the Royal Saloon, inquiring very minutely into the whole of the arrangement, and precisely at 12 o'clock the train left Slough for Paddington, Mr Gooch, the principal of the locomotive department, accompanied by Mr Brunel, the engineer, driving the engine.

At Paddington by 11 o'clock the centre of the wide space apportioned for the arrival of the incoming trains was parted off for the reception of the Royal and illustrious visitors, and covered by a crimson carpet, which reached from one end of the platform to the other; the whole of the arrangements for the reception of the Royal party being under the superintendence of Mr Seymour Clark, the superintendent of the line, assisted by Superintendent Collard, of the company's police.

Captain Hay, the Assistant Commissioner of Metropolitan Police, and Superintendent Lincoln and a large party of the D division, were also present. Before 12 o'clock, large numbers of elegantly-dressed ladies, consisting of the families and friends of the directors and officers of the company, were ranged on each side of the part apportioned for the arrival of the Royal train, and at five minutes before 12 o'clock, Her Majesty's carriage, drawn by four horses, arrived from the Royal Mews at Pimlico and a few minutes afterwards a detachment of the 8th Royal Irish Hussars, under the command of Captain Sir G Brown, arrived from the barracks at Kensington for the purpose of acting as an escort to Her Majesty.

Precisely at 25 minutes past 12 o'clock the Royal special train entered the Paddington terminus, having performed the distance in 25 minutes, and on Her Majesty alighting, she was received with the most deafening demonstrations of loyalty and affection we have ever experienced.

His Royal Highness Prince Albert alighted first. Her Majesty on being handed out of the Royal saloon, in a most condescending manner returned the gratulations of the assemblage present.

The cheers were re-echoed by the numerous persons who crowded the bridge over the terminus leading to Paddington Green, and lined the avenue towards the Junction Road, along which the Royal cavalcade passed. Her Majesty reached Buckingham Palace shortly before 1 o'clock, around which a large assemblage of respectable persons awaiting her arrival, by whom she was loudly feted.

The journey by rail took just 25 minutes, arriving at 12.25pm. The remainder of the journey by four-horse carriage through the London streets took half-an-hour.

The Firefly class 2-2-2 *Phlegethon*, built by Fenton, Murray & Jackson, entered service that year and ran in traffic until 1866. The name was later carried by a Hawthorn class locomotive. On one occasion, the queen travelled to Windsor in a Royal Train prepared by the GWR's rival the London & South Western Railway. However, she let it be known that she did not care for its dark blue furniture, and preferred the prettier pink decorations of the Great Western coaches. So the LSWR had to borrow the GWR Royal Train, and continued to do so for many years.

LSWR locoman George Lashman, who for 37 years was known as 'the Queen's engine driver', later related how on several occasions the queen stopped to have a long look at the locomotive pulling it.

Nearly 60 years after that first journey, after her funeral in 1901, Queen Victoria's coffin was taken to Paddington station and transported on the Royal Train.

CHAPTER ELEVEN

The Bristol & Exeter Railway

I T IS easy to look back at past centuries and wonder at the apparently slow rate of social, political or technological evolution. Trevithick showed in 1804 that it was possible to build a successful steam railway locomotive, yet he made no money from the concept and it took more than another two decades before we had the world's first public steam-hauled railway between Stockton-on-Tees and Darlington.

However, the opening of the Liverpool & Manchester Railway in 1830 lit the blue touchpaper and suddenly everyone wanted in on the act.

Within just two years of the GWR board engaging Brunel to build the first railway between London and Bristol, and before any part of the GWR main line was completed, he had already been appointed to build an adjoining line to take passengers on from Bristol to Exeter.

He was not even 30, yet Isambard was juggling many projects at the same time — any one of which would be more than a lifetime's achievement for any ordinary mortal. While his classic pieces of infrastructure at Maidenhead, Sonning and Box Hill were being designed, he was coming up with a blueprint for a separate 75½-mile line heading into south-west England.

The Bristol & Exeter Railway Company was incorporated on May 19,

1836, at the instigation of the GWR, and held its first meeting on July 26 that year. Formed by a group of Bristol merchants as early as November 1835, it was authorised to build a double track line between the two cities with branches to Weston-super-Mare and Tiverton.

The company appointed Brunel as consulting engineer and his broad gauge was chosen. Isambard selected the route for the line but his highly-trusted chief assistant William Gravatt, son of an assistant inspector of the Royal Military Academy who had worked with both Brunels on the Thames Tunnel, undertook much of the work.

The first section of the railway to be tackled covered the 33 miles from Bristol and Bridgwater, which was built by private contractors once legal wrangles over land acquisition had been sorted.

Major works on this section included a cutting through the western end of the Mendip Hills at Uphill near Weston, crossed by a remarkable brick 'flying bridge' designed by Brunel and known as Devil's Bridge, another through Puriton Hill on the northern edge of Bridgwater and a 100ft viaduct over the River Parrett on the Somerset Levels.

Here, Brunel's genius faltered somewhat. He tried to build a crossing over the River Parrett near Bridgwater with an arch that was even flatter than that of Maidenhead Bridge. This time the laws of physics were not as complaint. Movement of the foundations caused weakness and the structure, known as Somerset Bridge, was superseded with a timber version in 1843, which in turn was replaced by a steel girder bridge in 1904.

A major rift developed between Brunel and Gravatt over the railway's slow progress — with the former writing to the latter to express his lack of confidence in him. After Gravatt resigned, John Joseph Macdonnell stepped into his shoes.

The Bristol to Bridgwater line and the Weston-super-Mare branch opened to traffic on June 14, 1841. The first passengers were 400 invited guests aboard a private train hauled by Firefly class 2-2-2 *Fireball* and which took an hour and 45 minutes to reach Bridgwater from Bristol.

WESTON WAS TOO BRACING

The Weston branch was the first of Brunel's lines to serve a seaside resort. In decades to come, the GWR would become a byword for summer holidays in the south west. However, this 1¼-mile line had a somewhat unusual inception. Thanks to Weston residents' strong objections to steam engines, it had to be worked by horses.

With a severe lack of motive power up front, the gale-force winds which can turn Weston beach into a sandstorm within minutes often pushed the carriages along or held them back. One day, a boy in charge of the horse was reportedly hurled in front of a train as it was being blown along by the wind and killed.

Steam was eventually allowed into the resort, which began life as a sort of 'Bath-by-the-sea' destination for the well-to-do, and the original Weston branch and its station were superseded in 1884 by the present-day loop line. From June 30, once Box Tunnel was open, through running from Bridgwater to London began.

The Bristol & Exeter Railway extended to Taunton on July 1, 1842, the 11½-mile length largely following the valley of the River Tone. At Taunton, the river was straightened to avoid the need for two bridges close together. Next up was the 9¼-mile length between Taunton and a temporary railhead at Beambridge, two miles south of Wellington, which took until May 1, 1843, to complete.

Finally, the 21¾-mile Beambridge to Exeter section was opened on May 1, 1844, and included the 1092-yard Whiteball Tunnel on the summit of the line three miles south west of Wellington. On May 2, the *Exeter Flying Post*, reported on the opening:

The engineer under whom it has been constructed, I K Brunel Esq, FRS, in his construction of the Great Western Railway, boldly cast aside all prejudices and previous methods and like a wise man, profiting by experience, laid down a plan for himself. This method he has also adopted on the Bristol and Exeter line.

We can well recollect the strong and hostile feeling at the time was manifested to the system of proceedings recommended by Mr Brunel, but, happily, the Broad Gauge triumphed and the line of railway from London to Exeter is not surpassed in the world.

A newspaper is not the publication best calculated for entering into dry details and descriptions, relative to the formation and mechanism of a railway, but it may be observed, shortly, that the prepared timbers are laid down longitudinally, on which are fastened the rails by screws. Under the rail, however, is placed felt, or a thin layer of pieces of hardwood, and we observe that in the immediate neighbourhood of this city, to the one line of rail is attached felt, and to the other, pieces of hardwood. The beams of timber, to which the rails are thus attached, are tied together by cross pieces at certain intervals called transoms, which are strongly bolted to the longitudinal timbers.

By these methods, a degree of stability is given to the structure, and a speed has been attained such as has produced unqualified astonishment in all who have witnessed it, and we are entitled to say, that among the many benefits that mankind have derived from the combination of the discoveries of Science and the resources of Art, the facility and rapidity of intercommunication between distant centres of population and industry by the application of steam power on railways, stands out in prominent relief.

The most formidable work on the line from Bristol to Exeter, has been the Tunnel at White Ball Hill, 21 miles from Exeter. This is five-eighths of a mile in length, and, as is well known — to the Bristol side of the tunnel (the station at Beam Bridge) to which the line of the railway has for some time been completed. From that point through the tunnel to Exeter, the first engine, drawing trucks and heavily laden with timber, iron etc, came down on the afternoon of April 17, and continued making trips daily from Beam Bridge to Exeter, to the afternoon of the 24th instant, when Major General Pasley, inspector general of railways, met Mr Brunel, Dr Miller of this city, one of the directors, and other gentlemen officially connected with the line, at Beam Bridge and immediately proceeded to the inspection of the tunnel and the line thence to Exeter.

The inspection of the tunnel was by torchlight, and most minute, and we understand the Inspector General expressed his approbation of the manner in which this extraordinary work, by means of energy and skill, and considerable outlay, has been performed.

The inspection of the line was equally minute. The earthworks which in some parts are rather extensive — as in the neighbourhood of Rewe for instance — were examined with great attention; as also the various erections of masonry and brickwork and likewise, the several bridges, culverts and drains. Stafford bridge, between Stoke Canon and Exeter, being the point of junction of the rivers Exe and Culm was minutely inspected, and we understand, that by the engineers generally, an expression of its perfect adequacy and safety was pronounced.

At Cowley Bridge, the road from Exeter to Crediton, and North Devon is carried over the railway there by means of a skew bridge. This has a remarkable appearance, communication being intercepted by the railway at an oblique angle. The ease and smoothness of the entire line of road from Beam Bridge to Exeter was the theme of general admiration and approbation.

Describing the terminus, Exeter St David's station, the report said:

At the terminus are extensive ranges of buildings covering a very large area, the first of these at which the traveller arrives, on his left being the Departure Station, which is a parallelogram about 144ft in length — a structure present-ing considerable neatness in appearance, covered with slate and zinc. It is divided with every attention to the comfort and convenience of the public, and officers of the company, with all other necessary offices.

The Superintendent's room is next, with the Parcel Room adjoining and then is a spacious entrance way to the building. The Booking Office, a spacious and well-arranged room adjoins this and next is the Ladies' Waiting Room and the other requisite offices which occupy this range. These rooms all open into a spacious gallery the roof of which is carried over the line of rails, being supported in front by pillars and having a span of about 40ft.

Underneath this, the trains run, and passengers enter the several carriages from the gallery, which is parallel with the floors of the carriages. In line with this building is the situation of the two carriage sheds, each of which is about 100ft in length; the roofs of which are plank, with a covering of tarpaulin, and between these sheds is placed the turntable, a most ingenious and curious piece of mechanism on which are turned the several carriages.

Further on, and in line with these buildings is the Return Station, being a range of buildings, equal in extent to the Departure Station just described, with the booking office, etc, but not containing so many rooms. Within this area is a reservoir, the water requisite for which is supplied by the Exeter Water Company and a tank for the engines is in the course of erection. The station, offices etc, are lit with gas, supplied by the Exeter gas company.

On the right of the station is a vast building called the Goods Shed. This is 140ft in length and 66ft in width, having four windows on either side, and being roofed over with large slate. Lines of rail here are also carried through.

The report described a grand gala banquet in the goods warehouse which took place that day, attended by 800 people.

Firefly 2-2-2 *Actaeon* hauled the first train over the 388 miles from Paddington and back, and was driven by none other than Daniel Gooch. The average speed for the outbound five-hour journey inclusive of stops was 39mph, and on the way back he cut 20 minutes off the scheduled time, averaging 41½mph.

The world had up to then seen nothing like the speeds achieved on the Bristol & Exeter, which for a large part of its journey covered flat fen-like terrain. Paddington to Exeter express trains took just five hours, not days, as would have been the case a decade or more before, beginning on March 10, 1845. Even when an extra stop was added at Bridgwater, a further five minutes was cut off the journey.

The 9.50am Exeter-Paddington express which ran between 1847-52 was in its day the fastest train in the world. It was nicknamed 'The Flying Dutchman' after the racehorse that won the Derby and the St Leger in 1849.

Britain's railway network brought multiple benefits to provinces, not least of all the standardisation of time, which was often taken from the train guard's watch. At Exeter, an extra minute hand was added to a clock in Fore Street to show both railway time and local time.

For much of its life, the Bristol & Exeter was an extension of the GWR by the back door. Immediately on its opening, the railway was leased by the GWR for £70,000 a year, as to begin with it had no rolling stock or locomotives of its own.

That changed in 1849, when the Bristol & Exeter took over its own working, having turned down an offer by the GWR to buy it outright four years earlier. The company built its own carriage works at Bridgwater, and ordered its own fleet of engines, 10 each from Stothert & Slaughter of Bristol and Longridge & Co from Bedlington. They were all smaller versions of Gooch's GWR Iron Duke class.

The next step in its independence was to build locomotive workshops at Temple Meads, and in 1859 it produced the first of 23 broad gauge engines of its own there. The works became known as Bristol Bath Road, which acquired fame as a steam depot in the next century.

Many Brunel projects had exceeded their budgets, mainly due to his grandiose structures. Yet the Bristol & Exeter cost less than the £2 million allocated for its construction. It went on to become a considerable financial success and between 1844 and 1874 paid an average annual dividend of 4.5% — opening branches to Clevedon, Tiverton, Yeovil, Chard, Portishead, Wells via Cheddar, Barnstaple and Minehead. However, the city authorities in Exeter refused to allow the company to build a freight spur into the dock of the Exeter Canal until 35 years after it entered the city in 1844.

During 1854-61, the Bristol & Exeter leased the Somerset Central Railway from Burnham to Wells. That line subsequently merged with the Dorset Central to become the Somerset & Dorset Railway. In 1867, the BER laid a mixed gauge along the main line from Highbridge to Bridgwater in a vain attempt to keep the Somerset & Dorset away from the latter.

The Bristol & Exeter also harboured Brunelian transatlantic dreams of its own. In the 1860s, the railway made plans to turn the limestone promontory of Brean Down into a major port, and went as far as laying a foundation stone on November 5, 1864. The company was, however, more easily deterred than Isambard. The next day, the fierce Bristol Channel currents carried the buoy to which the stone had been attached far away, and the harbour scheme quickly crumbled.

The inevitable happened on January 1, 1876, when the Bristol & Exeter was fully amalgamated with the GWR.

CHAPTER TWELVE

South Devon: Taking it to the limit and beyond

W E HAVE seen how the first half of the GWR route from London to Bristol was described as 'Brunel's billiard table' because the ruling gradient was all but flat, and how world steam speed records for timetabled trains were established on the Bristol & Exeter Railway largely because of its level terrain.

Striking south from Exeter was, however, a different matter, as indeed would be the entire south-west peninsula beyond the city. The gentleness of Berkshire and Oxfordshire terrain was a dramatic contrast to the rugged countryside of Devon and Cornwall, in particular the coastal route from Exeter to Newton Abbot chosen by Brunel and the foothills of Dartmoor thereafter.

This midget of a man – he stood just 5ft 3in tall – more than made up for his physical stature in the world of engineering, a field in which he towered as a giant above most if not all others of his day. Time and time again, he tore up the rule book and started again with a blank sheet to work out just how far the laws of nature and physics could be pushed.

In South Devon, however, Brunel was to discover exactly where those limitations lay. The South Devon Railway was formed to build a line running 52 miles from Exeter to Plymouth and received its royal assent on July 4, 1844.

Isambard had made no secret of his desire to see his broad gauge stretch all the way to Penzance, and was appointed by the South Devon as engineer, in view of his immense success on the GWR, Bristol & Exeter and other connecting railways.

Isambard's initial surveys of possible routes westwards showed a seemingly endless number of sharp gradients which could be problematic for the steam trains of the day, even if Dartmoor and its foothills were bypassed. Hemerdon, Dainton and Rattery — names which were to pass into railway folklore — each featured gradients which had to be tackled if Plymouth was to be linked by rail to Paddington.

Top of Brunel's list of ideas was — if the steam locomotive can't do it, get rid of the steam locomotive! At the time, Britain's national rail network was just beginning to come together, and by then steam was regarded almost universally as the undoubted path to the future. Yet in seeking the best, Brunel would show scant regard for what others believed.

He and his father Marc had worked on an alternative to the steam locomotive for a decade, convinced that they could do better. The project, known as the Gaz Engine, began in 1824 and involved a locomotive running on carbonic acid gas. Scientists Humphry Davy and Michael Faraday found that several gases could be liquefied at low temperature and under high pressure, and Marc Brunel believed that the principle could better the steam locomotive concept.

He came up with a design in which a double-acting piston moved backwards and forwards in an oil-filled metal cylinder. On either side were two pairs of pressure vessels, one of each pair filled with pressurised carbonic gas, and the other with oil which would perform the function of transferring changes of pressure. Changing the state of the gas would drive the piston up and down. The principle could be used to turn an axle.

Isambard persevered with the Gaz Engine until January 1833, when he sadly concluded that it could offer no advantages in fuel economy over the steam locomotive. As we have seen, steam locomotives were Isambard's weak spot, and it was his sidekick Daniel Gooch who had saved the day for the GWR in this respect. That did not stop Brunel from looking elsewhere for new forms of traction though.

THE ATMOSPHERIC RAILWAY

After being appointed as engineer on the South Devon Railway, Isambard did not have to look very hard. In September 1844, he and Gooch along with other leading engineers of the day witnessed a demonstration by inventors Samuel Clegg and Jacob Samuda of an atmospheric train on the one and a half mile long Dalkey & Kingstown Railway — which ran between Kingstown Harbour with the Dublin & Dalkey Railway.

Samuda, a marine engineering expert, had joined forces with Clegg, a gas lighting pioneer, to devise and patent the atmospheric system of propulsion on January 3, 1838. Their technology consisted of a cast-iron tube laid between rails and sealed by airtight valves at each end. A piston linked to the bottom of a carriage was pushed past the vale into the tube, and stationary steam engines on the side of the railway pumped air out of the tube, creating a vacuum ahead of the piston. The greater pressure of the atmosphere behind the piston would force it along the tube and pull the carriage with it, without any need for a locomotive.

Not only that, but atmospheric traction did not rely on the adhesion of heavy locomotives to the rails. All you would need to do to counteract steep gradients would be to increase the diameter of the vacuum pipe, add a second pipe, or just build another or a bigger pumping station. Steeper inclines were therefore possible, and big savings could be made on earthworks.

This was the answer staring Isambard in the face, or so he thought. Gooch, however, was far from convinced, and pointed out that in the case of the Irish railway, it would be cheaper to use steam locomotives. He was backed in this view by none other than Robert Stephenson.

Isambard would not hear any of it. Prime Minister Sir Robert Peel backed his enthusiasm for the atmospheric system and wanted to see all railways converted to the principle. At the time of Railway Mania in the 1840s, new railway schemes were seen by speculators as a licence to print money. Railway shares were soaring on a daily basis, and those who proposed building atmospheric lines had little difficulty in finding funding.

Following hard on the heels of the Irish demonstration line came the London & Croydon in 1846, extending to 7½ miles from Croydon to New Cross in London, and the 1.4-mile Paris & St-Germain Railway in 1847.

Brunel too recommended the adoption of a proposal from Clegg and Samuda to install atmospheric propulsion over the whole length of the proposed South Devon Railway. Enticed by the prospect of money being saved, the directors gave his plan their unanimous approval. Isambard then headed straight to his time-honoured drawing board, where once again his Great Western imagination went into overdrive. In his typical flamboyant architectural style, he drew up plans for massive Italianate engine houses to stand at three-mile intervals along the route from Exeter to Teignmouth, to create the vacuum.

The adoption of atmospheric propulsion over such a long line was radical enough, but Brunel designed this first section of route to run at the foot of the soaring sandstone cliffs where South Devon meets the Atlantic Ocean, almost on the high-tide mark. Was this the mark of an engineering genius, or just plainly absurd?

The stunningly picturesque line would — as many future generations would see — totter on the thin dividing line between the devil and the deep blue sea, as it darted through a series of short tunnels linking red-sand beaches and romantic coves. To the west stood the cliffs, where rockfalls are a persistent menace to this day, while to the east lay the sea, where rough weather would shower the line in spray and storm surges send waves crashing over it. Locals were not entirely convinced, and nicknamed the project 'the Atmospheric caper'.

Nine pumping houses were built, at Exeter St Davids, Countess Wear, Turf Locks, Starcross, Dawlish, Bishopsteignton, Newton Abbot, Totnes, and one at Torre in Torquay to serve a projected branch line to the resort. However, Brunel quickly found out that the atmospheric propulsion technology in which he had placed so many of his hopes was still very much in its infancy, at least regarding a line of this length.

Early tests showed that the planned 12in vacuum pipe needed to be replaced by one of 15in diameter. Accordingly, the stationary pumping engines already installed along the route had to run faster than their design speed in order to maintain the vacuum. And it was not just in South Devon that such problems were encountered. Was Isambard really unaware of the problems that led to the closure of the London & Croydon atmospheric railway after only a year? If he was aware, and even without the benefits of telephone communication or the internet in those days, it is difficult to believe that he did not know, why did he not let the South Devon directors know? The atmospheric apparatus was still being stalled when the first section of the South Devon Railway was opened on May 30, 1846, using steam engines.

Two public atmospheric trains ran over the line on September 13, 1847, and from January 10, 1848, vacuum-powered services were extended to Newton Abbot, with some freight being carried too. Brunel was right about the high speeds which atmospheric trains could reach.

One train hit 68mph with a 28-ton load and 35mph with 100 tons. However, the 20-mile journey from Exeter to Newton Abbot with four stops took a slow 55 minutes with one train having to wait for the other to pass as the route was still single track. Another big problem was that while the scientific principles of atmospheric propulsion may have appeared sound on paper, in reality it was very different.

The hinge of the airtight valve and the ring around the piston were both made of leather, an organic material which was totally unsuitable for the purpose, as had just proved to be the case at Croydon. Had modern synthetic materials been available at the time, the problem might never have arisen.

The solution here was to have a large team of men permanently on hand to run a sticky sealant on the valve to make it airtight. Labour costs therefore rose dramatically at a stroke. Then the sealant proved useless after exposure to the air, so a new compound using cod-liver oil and soap was tried — but in vain. This compound, along with natural oils in the leather, was sucked into the vacuum pipe, and the leather dried and cracked in the sun, wind and salty air. The leather was also said to have been gnawed by rats.

Air leaked into the pipe through the cracks in the leather and so the steam pumps had to work much harder and burn more coal to keep up the pressure in the pipe. It was also discovered that the vacuum pipes had been cast too roughly, while the stationary steam engine pumps kept breaking down. Finally, a letter from a member of the public drew the directors' attention to the costly problem with the leather. While the problems mounted, Isambard had been noticeably absent from Devon.

It was shown that it cost 37 pence to run an atmospheric train for a mile as opposed to just 16 pence for steam. Gooch and Robert Stephenson had been proved right. In desperation, the directors along with GWR chairman Charles Russell visited Isambard at his house at 18 Duke Street in London in a bid to get answers. Isambard admitted that the pumping stations lacked sufficient power, but blamed the other failings on Clegg & Samuda.

Regardless of the cost, the atmospheric railway successfully ran nine trains a day between Exeter and Teignmouth during spring and summer 1848, at average speeds of 64mph. However, when the trains broke down third-class passengers were asked to get out and push.

Brunel told the directors that they needed to replace the pumps and the pipes but his answer was not satisfactory. They were prepared to back the atmospheric system with their money no longer and reverted to steam haulage from September 10, 1848, while giving Clegg and Samuda a last chance to repair the airtight valve.

On August 29 that year, Isambard was man enough to face down furious South Devon shareholders at a meeting in Plymouth and say that he had got it wrong about atmospheric propulsion. He agreed to waive his fee for building the line until it opened throughout to Plymouth, which it did on April 2, 1849, using steam engines despite the notorious gradients, having reached Totnes on June 20, 1847, minus atmospheric trains, and a temporary terminus at Laire on the city's outskirts on May 5, 1848. Meanwhile, the Kingstown atmospheric system closed in 1854 and the Paris line in 1860.

The South Devon Railway company built its offices outside Plymouth station and extended its line into the new Plymouth Great Western Docks in 1850. Three years later, it opened a branch to the older Plymouth harbour at Sutton Pool by converting a part of the horse-worked Plymouth & Dartmoor Railway to broad gauge.

A branch was opened from Newton Abbot to Torquay on December 18, 1848. This line was extended as the independent Dartmouth & Torbay Railway on August 2, 1859, finally reaching Kingswear on August 1864. All were built to broad gauge. The South Devon Railway was amalgamated with the GWR on February 1, 1876.

Had modern-day materials been available, it is probable that solutions would have been found to many of the problems that beset the atmospheric railway. Then again, the later development of the steam locomotive and its diesel replacement would probably have negated any benefits that the atmospheric system had to offer.

Today's answer to Brunel's perceived problems would have been electrification. For me, there is little doubt that if he is looking down on Network Rail now, his only question about electrifying his original main line would be — why has it taken you so long?

BRITAIN'S COSTLIEST RAILWAY LINE

The route of the South Devon Railway from Exeter to Teignmouth has always been described as one of the loveliest in Britain, because of its spectacular coastal panoramas. Thanks to Brunel's decision to build it at the base of cliffs, it is also one of the most expensive to maintain. Not only that, but if it becomes blocked, there is no other way of getting from Plymouth to Exeter by train.

Two alternative routes once existed. The GWR had the Teign Valley Line, which ran from Newton Abbot via Heathfield to Exeter, but passenger services were withdrawn in 1958 and the line was closed between Christow and Exeter from 1961 as a result of flooding, and then cut back progressively.

The Southern Railway's main line from Exeter to Plymouth was closed in May 1968, with the section between Bere Alston and Meldon Quarry near Okehampton lifted. These closure decisions left all the eggs in one basket, a situation which persists today.

The maintenance of the Dawlish sea wall route has always been problematic, because of cliff falls and sea surges. In December 1852 a slippage east of Teignmouth closed the railway for four days, and in 1855 and 1859, the sea cut through the tracks at the resort.

The GWR proposed building an avoiding line in 1935, went as far as buying up parcels of land for it. The nine-mile route ran from Newton Abbot, leaving the existing main line near the Hackney Canal and junction with the Teign Valley line, and rejoined the original route north of Dawlish Warren station. A longer route between Exminster and Bishopsteignton had also been mooted.

The scheme was approved by Parliament in 1936. The GWR then sought further powers to extend the avoiding line by seven miles to the north, rejoining the coastal route at Exminster just south of Exeter. An Act empowering this 'extension' was passed in 1937. Surveying began in 1937, and the avoiding line was scheduled to open within two years. However, after the Nazis invaded Poland and the Second World War commenced, all that changed. The plans were scuppered and never revived.

In recent times there have been calls to rebuild the Southern Railway main line between Exeter and Plymouth, joining the Dartmoor Railway at Okehampton to Network Rail's Tamar Valley Line at Bere Alston, as a diversionary route. However, critics say that it would bypass the main centres of population in South Devon. In 2010, Parliament heard that around £9 million had been invested on keeping the sea wall safe and the cliff faces stable in recent times, and its maintenance costs Network Rail around £500,000 each year. On November 28, 2012, more than 1500 tons of debris between Sprey Point and Parsons Tunnel cascaded on to the line between Exeter and Newton Abbot, blocking it for three days.

Devon-based independent transport expert Neill Mitchell has called for a fresh look to be taken at the GWR's 'Dawlish Avoiding Line' plans. He said that modern-day tunnelling technology could facilitate a more direct high-speed route between Exeter and Newton Abbot, possibly beneath Haldon Hill. He believes that the coastal route should remain open only for local stopping trains and the times when it would need to be used as a diversionary route itself, during engineering work on the new line.

"It is simply not acceptable for the 21st century business, freight, tourism and leisure rail service in the peninsula to remain dependent on a solitary fairweather railway," he said.

However, in 2019, Network Rail published updated proposals to move a mile-long section of the line between Parsons Tunnel, near Holcombe, and Teignmouth slightly out to sea and realign the railway away from the hazardous cliffs. Such a move would more than likely mean the end of any plans to open an alternative route inland or reopen the Okehampton and Tavistock route.

The beauty of Brunel's South Devon Railway is not only in the eye of the beholder, but in the pocket of the taxpayer too.

THE BRUNELS ON HOLIDAY

As previously stated, one of the GWR's greatest claims to fame was its ability to provide speedy travel to seaside resorts for the mass of the working population who saw social conditions radically improve towards the end of the Victorian age, combined with statutory paid holidays.

Following the opening of the Bristol & Exeter Railway, the first rail-borne tourists began to arrive; among them was an elderly Marc Brunel and his wife, carried there by their son's railways.

Tourism by train to Exeter itself began to be big business from 1850 onwards, and paved the way for the GWR and its rival the LSWR to open up the West Country as Britain's premier home destination for summer holidays. Isambard also had his eye on the English Rivera as his ideal place to live, after his family spent many holidays there.

From July to November 1848, he and his wife Mary stayed at Vomero, a Grade II listed Victorian villa in Stitchill Road, Torquay. They were making arrangements to move into a far bigger property in the nearby village of Watcombe. Isambard designed a manor house, now known as Brunel Manor, as a retirement home, after buying a plot of land. However, he did not live to see the planned house and gardens completed. The house was eventually completed, to a different design, by paper manufacturer James Crompton. Today, it is owned by The Woodlands House of Prayer Trust and used as a Christian holiday, retreat and conference centre.

CHAPTER THIRTEEN

Paddington through the ages

S TUPENDOUS NATURE-DEFYING bridges, flamboyant neo-classical station architecture, cavernous tunnels, yawning chasms of cuttings, a wave-lashed route between the devil and the deep blue sea, world speed records... it seemed that Brunel's Big Railway had it all.

Where it fell down was the starting point. As built, the first GWR Paddington station in Bishop's Bridge Road was a basic functional affair, surrounded by green fields, on the western edge of London.

This was the gateway to North America, where you could buy a ticket and hop on a train and then a steamship to travel to New York. For the less adventurous, a fast trip to the West Country would have been more commonplace.

Bristol Temple Meads was magnificent from the start, even though it was rapidly enlarged to cope with mushrooming levels of traffic and then superseded by the structure we have today. Yet by comparison, the London terminus was very much a Cinderella affair, built on the cheap. Its four platforms were covered by a plain wooden arched truss-roofed trainshed open to the elements at both sides.

Everyone, including Brunel, knew only too well that it had to go to the ball. It was a waiting game for the time when sufficient funds would be ready to build a terminus fit for the capital. And it was a long time coming. The GWR had outgrown Paddington, where its headquarters had been established, by the 1840s, but the cost-conscious board of directors were cautious about parting with a vast sum of money to replace it.

When the Railway Mania collapsed in 1847, just as the dot com bubble did in the 21st century, and dividends had to be lowered, the purse strings were pulled even tighter. Yet there was no hiding the fact that the original station, the face of the GWR in one of the world's busiest cities, and where traffic levels were far higher than when the line opened, had long since been fit for purpose. Passengers knew it too, and it was obvious that the railway could lose out to competitors.

The GWR ran its first public excursion in 1844, from London to Bath, Bristol, Taunton and Exeter. Excursion traffic was to become big business for both the GWR and Paddington, and few will forget the summer Saturday scenes of the early and mid-20th century when the platforms were packed with holidaymakers waiting to head to the West Country or Wales.

On December 21, 1850, Isambard received his Christmas present four days early. The board had given the green light for a new station to be built.

He had been patiently waiting for the day, and already had a drawer full of preliminary sketches to hand. His design involved a 10-track trainshed 700ft long and 238ft wide in the triangle between Praed Street and Eastbourne Terrace. Five of the tracks would serve platforms and the other five were to be stock sidings.

This time, Brunel did not look back to ancient Greece or Rome for his inspiration, but a few miles to the south to the plans for the gigantic glasshouse that was to become Crystal Palace, designed by Joseph Paxton and built for the Great Exhibition of 1851. It became a global landmark overnight, and Brunel wanted his new Paddington to be exactly the same. His blueprint included spectacular wrought-iron arched roof spans supported by two rows of cylindrical columns cast-iron columns, while his friend Matthew Digby Wyatt designed the ironwork for the ornate glass screens at the west end of the station. Paxton's patent glazing was used for the roof lights.

Brunel also worked with the contractor Fox, Henderson, & Co on the design. Brunel, Paxton, Wyatt, and Sir Charles Fox met while the Crystal Palace was being built. Months before the Crystal Palace was finished, Brunel wrote to Wyatt, saying:

I am going to design, in a great hurry, a station after my own fancy... with engineering roofs etc, etc.

It is at Paddington, in a cutting, and admitting of no exterior, all interior and all roofed in.

Now such a thing will be entirely metal as to all the general forms, arrangements and design; it almost of necessity becomes an Engineering Work, but, to be honest, even if it were not, it is a branch of architecture of which I am fond, and, of course, believe myself to be fully competent for, but for detail of ornamentation I neither have time nor knowledge, and with all my confidence in my own ability I have never any objection to advice and assistance even in the department which I keep to myself, namely the general design.

Now, in this building which, entre nous, will be one of the largest of its class, I want to carry out, strictly and fully, all those correct notions of the use of metal which I believe you and I share (except that I should carry them still farther than you).

The first train left the new Paddington on January 16, 1854. The main roof had still not been completed, and it would be another four months before the new arrival platforms became operational. Yet the new station was certainly worth the wait, and the expense. After it opened, the original station it superseded became the site of the goods depot, with sidings along the Grand Union Canal.

The first all-mail train from Paddington ran in 1855. Three years later, slip coaches were used for the first time, where portions of a train could be detached at various points and taken onwards separately over connecting routes.

The Great Western Hotel was built in front of the station in Praed Street during 1851-1854. GWR director George Burke came up with the idea that a luxury hotel should be built to serve the new showpiece terminus. It was designed by architect Philip Charles Hardwick, son of Philip

Hardwick, who designed the Euston Arch for the London & Birmingham, later London & North Western Railway terminus into which Brunel's Big Railway was originally intended to run. He designed it in the renaissance style of the French King Louis XIV, giving it a chateau-like appearance, with sculpture by John Thomas.

That company had emerged as a rival to the GWR, and already had two hotels at Euston. Money might be short, but the Paddington empire could not afford to trail behind. Like the station behind it, a magnificent structure arose, with 112 bedrooms, 15 sitting rooms, lounges, restaurants and public rooms. Little wonder it was so grandiose — for the chairman of the hotel company was none other than Isambard.

The Great Western Royal Hotel was formally opened on June 8, 1854, by Prince Albert, the Royal Consort, and his guest the King of Portugal. The hotel was a dazzling success, and set the standard for similar luxury accommodation throughout Britain. It was taken over by the GWR and remodelled between 1936 and 1938.

AN EVOLVING DESIGN

As traffic increased, it was only natural that the GWR's principal terminus would evolve with it. The GWR empire kept expanding not only by building new main lines and branches of its own, but absorbing adjoining railways. All of this increased demand on the principal destination, Paddington, where local commuter traffic was also booming.

Signalboxes and semaphore signals appeared in the 1860s, and the first through train from Paddington to Penzance ran in 1867. Station offices were added in 1881, and four years later, more departure platforms were added, with extra arrival platforms opening in 1893. Platforms took the place of carriage sidings, and turntables were taken out from the part of the concourse known as The Lawn.

In 1882, postal parcels were carried by the GWR for the first time, and the following year, the company set up its own goods collection and delivery services. The station had to be expanded with a surge in traffic by the early part of the 20th century too.

Nonstop services had been established between Paddington and Bristol and Newport in 1896, and between Paddington and Birmingham Snow Hill three years later. The first nonstop 'Cornish Riviera' express from Paddington to Penzance ran on July 1, 1904. The West of England route to Penzance became shorter as Brunel's original railway was improved by replacing certain sections with short cuts in 1906, and four years later, a shorter route to Birmingham was opened.

There was also the opening of the line to Fishguard Harbour, a new gateway to Ireland. Under Gooch's 20th century successors such as George Jackson Churchward and Charles B Collett, GWR locomotive technology took massive strides forward, with the knock-on effect that Paddington became even busier. By 1911, the total face length was 8285ft, as opposed to the 3500ft of the original. A new roof span built from steel as opposed to wrought iron was completed and a fourth span was erected in 1915. Platforms 9 to 12 were added in 1916. The running lines out to the GWR's Old Oak Common depot were also realigned.

After the First World War, the station was expanded still further. The cast-iron roof columns were replaced by steel ones. Colour light signals came in 1922, and electrically-worked signalboxes in 1933.

As a job creation exercise in the Great Depression, the platforms were lengthened, The Lawn cleared and a new concourse developed, with new offices built. Bishop's Road station, which had been a separate stop on the Metropolitan Line, was absorbed into Paddington and became its suburban platforms. By 1931, there were 201 departures a day, compared to just 20 in 1855.

Brunel's design had become one of the finest termini in the world by the outbreak of the Second World War. Accordingly, it became a prime target for the Luftwaffe, with 400 incidents but just one serious strike — when a bomb burst one of the roof ribs in 1944.

PADDINGTON POSTWAR

Paddington saw out the steam age largely unaltered since before the war. Only after the end of steam on British Railways were more major improvements made to Paddington. They included, between 1985-92, the complete restoration of Isambard's triple-span roof, while platforms six, seven and eight were realigned and remodelled. The culmination of the scheme did much to restore its original glory as Brunel intended.

Further major development works took place between 1995-98 when overhead electrification was installed on platforms three to 12 and the footbridge between platforms six and 10 was rebuilt. This was carried out in preparation for the introduction of the Heathrow Express service, and gave a foretaste of the electrification of the entire route to Bristol and beyond.

In the 21st century, Network Rail drew up plans to demolish the arched section to the north-east of Paddington station, known as Span 4 – the extension completed in 1916 on which the roof had become dangerous. In the 1990s, it was even deemed necessary to install an internal blanket to protect people from falling glass.

Span 4 was to be replaced by an office block over the rails – but conservationists protested, saying that although it was not part of Brunel's original station it had a heritage value of its own. It was subsequently decided that it would be restored. That happened between 2009 and 2010 at a cost of £35 million, with platforms nine to 12 also fully restored. The span reopened in late 2011, looking markedly brighter than the other three spans.

Today, Paddington with its 14 platforms handles inter-city services to Oxford, Bristol, Bath, Exeter, Plymouth, Cornwall, Worcester, Hereford, Cardiff and Swansea, and occasionally Birmingham services when Marylebone is unavailable, and also commuter trains to Slough, Maidenhead, Reading and Swindon and while the Heathrow Express services link it to Heathrow Airport.

Paddington is also served by the Bakerloo, Circle, District and Hammersmith & City lines of London Underground, and has undergone a third major phase with the completion of the £14.9 billion Crossrail scheme, Europe's biggest civil engineering project of the present day.

Crossrail, a new 21st century line 73 miles long, links Berkshire and Buckinghamshire via Greater London to Essex and Kent with 31 miles of new east-to-west tunnels. Ten-car trains will run at frequencies of up to 24 trains per hour in each direction through the central tunnel section taking the route from Paddington to Whitechapel, with further tunnelling to Stratford and to Canary Wharf.

The central section tunnels begin at a portal just west of Paddington, where a new station had been built underneath the GWR terminus serving Crossrail, overground and London Underground lines. The idea of boring new large-diameter tunnels beneath London to link Paddington and Liverpool Street overground stations was proposed by railwayman George Dow in the London evening newspaper *The Star* on June 14, 1941, but after numerous ideas were drawn up, it was not until July 22, 2008 that the Crossrail Act received Royal Assent.

Eight 7.1m diameter tunnel-boring machines ordered from Herrenknecht AG of Germany for the work were all named by competition winners in early 2012. The two machines used on the Plumstead to North Woolwich section, ironically digging a new Thames Tunnel, were named *Mary* and *Sophia*, after the wives of Marc and Isambard Brunel.

The machines represent technology that in those now-distant days of picks and shovels the Brunels may never have even dreamed of, but of which they most certainly would have approved, as they would have done about Crossrail. Isambard would have surely jumped at the chance to head that company.

The proposed High Speed 2 railway, linking London to Birmingham and later Manchester, Leeds and eventually Scotland through new purpose-built super-fast routes, would see train running at speeds of up to 250mph. Travellers could get from London, where HS2 would link to Crossrail, to Birmingham in 49 minutes, or be in Manchester in just over an hour.

Many reports about HS2, especially those that are favourable in tone, have cited Isambard Brunel as an inspiration for the scheme. While there is a sizeable body of opposition to HS2, largely for environmental reasons, and the loss of properties, some historic, which will have to be demolished, proponents said this is just what Brunel would have done – the greater end justifying the means. Indeed, just as Brunel's Big Railway slashed journey times from Paddington to Bristol and the West Country to a fraction of the time it took by stagecoach, so HS2 was designed to make the cities of the Midlands and north attractively commutable to London. Brunel, a man who cut through obstacles in his way with renowned ingenuity, would certainly have approved... or would he?

Serious questions have been regularly raised as to just how much HS2 will benefit the nation. In early 2020, fears were sounded that the total cost would soar to £106 billion, as compared to an initial budget estimate of just £355 million. There are already frequent fast main line services between these cities, and while HS2 would markedly slash journey times, where is the demand?

In late 2012, five air services a day were introduced from Leeds Bradford International to London, but were soon cut to three in accordance with public demand. They offered a total of 200 seats a day, whereas HS2 would offer 600 seats every half hour, so where will the demand come from? How many people want to commute from Leeds to London on a daily basis, even if they could afford airline-level ticket prices?

At the same time as modern transport technology is developing, the internet is evolving even faster. And the switch to home-working driven by the COVID-19 pandemic is likely to have curtailed whatever demand there was for the scheme still further. Why travel hundreds of miles at great expense if you can simply log into your company's systems remotely and speak to your colleagues using video conferencing software?

Maybe we remain on the cusp a new age of Brunellian railway building, or perhaps it will be overtaken by another form of technology, just as Isambard forced stagecoaches out of business.

CHAPTER FOURTEEN

The conquest of Cornwall

T HE WHOLE world changed in Cornwall at the dawn of the 19th century. In what was a hotbed of heavy industry in the form of the tin and copper industry, mining engineer Richard Trevithick devised a self-propelled steam locomotive which would run on roads. When he found out that the muddy potholed roads of the day would not carry its weight, he looked instead to railways, which hitherto had been worked by horses. In 1804, two years before Isambard Brunel was born, he gave his first public demonstration of a steam locomotive on the Penydarren Tramroad near Merthyr Tydfil.

Cornwall had to wait another 30 years for its first steam railway however, when the Bodmin & Wadebridge was opened.

Three years later, on December 23, 1837, the standard gauge Hayle Railway, partially worked by steam, partially by horses and rope-worked inclined planes, opened to take copper and tin ore from the Redruth and Camborne mining heartland to the ports of Hayle and Redruth.

Passengers were carried on its main line between Hayle and Redruth from May 22, 1843, with intermediate stations at Pool, Camborne, Penponds, Gwinear, Angarrack, Copperhouse and Hayle Riviere. By the Whitsun bank holiday, it was running seaside excursions.

THE WEST CORNWALL RAILWAY

The Hayle Railway proved so successful that local businessmen looked at extending it at either end, to Penzance and Truro, and formed the West Cornwall Railway company. They proposed using the atmospheric system between Redruth and Truro.

After a first parliamentary bill was defeated in 1845, a second received the royal assent on August 3, 1846. It also gave the new company powers to buy the Hayle Railway, which happened on November 3 that year, and to build deviations to eliminate the inclined planes, and to complete the route between Penzance and Truro.

The line was to be built to broad gauge but at first, because of the collapse of Railway Mania, it was difficult to raise the necessary finance. When the money did become available, it was decided to go for standard gauge in order to save the expense of rebuilding the Hayle Railway. However, parliamentary powers obtained in 1850 were conditional on the West Cornwall laying 7ft 0¼in gauge rails on six months' notice from any connecting broad gauge line.

While working on the Midland Railway main line, engineer William Henry Barlow established that the replacement of rotten sleepers was a large part of the cost of track maintenance. To combat this problem, he patented his own design of rail in 1849. Its wide flanged profile could be laid directly onto track ballast without the need for sleepers. Barlow rail, as it became known, was widely used on the GWR broad gauge and associated lines.

Brunel was appointed as engineer to the West Cornwall and it was built using cost-saving Barlow rails. Where viaducts were needed, they were built to Brunel's timber trestle design, which had been successful in crossing deep valleys in South Devon. Brunel had built his first timber bridge across Sonning Cutting, a five-span structure which carried a public road. A far cry from Hanworth viaduct and Maidenhead bridge, nine trestle bridges were built on the West Cornwall, allowing the deep valleys of the far west to be crossed as cheaply and economically as possible.

The route between Redruth and Penzance was almost ready by February 1852 and then connection was made with the Hayle Railway. A locomotive was first seen in Penzance station on February 25, and two days later the chairman made a trial inspection run over the line, which opened on March 11, 1852, at first operating three trains a day.

The railway reached Higher Town on the western side of Truro on August 25, 1852, with an extension to Newham within the city limits following on April 16, 1855. The West Cornwall provided easier travel to London for those living at the far end of the duchy for the first time. Before the coming of the railway, the best means of travel to and from the capital was by sea: the roads were poor or nonexistent.

After the railway was opened, passengers could travel from Penzance or Truro to Hayle, take the paddle steamer packet service to Bristol and travel eastwards via the GWR.

THE CORNWALL RAILWAY

Falmouth, an important shipping port, also wanted in on the railway revolution but several early schemes to link it to London by rail came to nothing. In 1843, in advance of the South Devon Railway being completed, local businessmen W Tweedy and W H Bond asked the GWR to fund an extension of it into Cornwall.

The GWR told them to promote an independent scheme, and a prospectus for the Cornwall Railway was duly produced in 1844. It was to cross the Hamoaze, the tidal estuary of the Tamar at Torpoint, by ferry, and run via Liskeard, Lostwithiel, Par and St Austell to Truro and Falmouth. The GWR, Bristol & Exeter and South Devon and Bristol & Gloucester railways each subscribed to the tune of £250,000.

The engineer appointed was soldier Captain William Scarth Moorsom, who had built the famous Lickey Incline on the Birmingham & Gloucester Railway. That company found Isambard Brunel's plan to climb the Lickeys, which involved stationary engines hauling trains up by cable, too expensive, and took a chance on Moorsom's cheaper but by no means guaranteed use of steam locomotives. Indeed, even up to the end of the steam age trains still used a 'Lickey banker' locomotive to help push them over the top.

However, when the House of Lords rejected the Cornwall Railway scheme because of the Hamoaze ferry component, Brunel was brought in as engineer to build a bridge across the Tamar. He chose a spot two miles north of Torpoint and his broad gauge Cornwall Railway scheme duly received royal assent on August 3, 1846.

By now the Railway Mania bubble had burst and there was no money to build the line, although some work was done near St Austell. Brunel came back with a scaled-down plan, under which the line could be built to single track for far less money. In April 1852 the directors came up with a capital reconstruction of the scheme which saw the 37-mile length between Truro, where it met the West Cornwall Railway, and Plymouth being started. In January 1853, a £162,000 contract for building the bridge over the Tamar was let.

However, money ran short in a financial depression when shareholders defaulted on their subscriptions, and the consortium of the GWR, Bristol & Exeter and South Devon railways agreed to lease the line in return for guaranteeing bank loans.

Building of the railway again necessitated crossing numerous deep valleys. There were so many of these that there was neither the time nor the money for Brunel to come up with grandiose schemes for each. Again, his utilitarian timber trestle viaducts did the job, but these were a short-term gain and long-term loss as they suffered from heavy maintenance costs.

Following the pattern of the 670ft-long Ivybridge Viaduct on the South Devon and also the 1760ft Landore Viaduct in South Wales, he built 34 viaducts over the 53 miles between Plymouth and Truro, each built in timber and supported on masonry pillars. They were also known as fan viaducts because of the shape of the supports.

Answering criticism that the Baltic pine they were built from could rot away, he designed the trestle bridges and viaducts so that decaying timbers could be unbolted and replaced Meccano-style without having to close the railway. Accordingly, several of these viaducts lasted for 60 years, although others were replaced by masonry structures towards the end of the 19th century. It was only when the price of timber soared during the First World War that there was a renewed urgency to replace them.

THE ROYAL ALBERT BRIDGE

On the banks of the Tamar, long held to be the 'great divide' between Cornwall and the rest of Britain, Isambard Kingdom Brunel was faced with yet another insurmountable obstacle, a river estuary 1100ft wide and 70ft deep. At first he tried to play it safe with a conventional bridge.

Cost conscious by now, he drew up plans for a timber bridge with one main span of 255ft and six further spans of 105ft each. The Royal Navy was not happy, because tall ships were then the order of the day, and demanded that any bridge must allow at least 100ft headroom so they could safely pass below.

Brunel then produced a radical blueprint that involved a single-span bridge to clear the estuary in one go, but at a price. The estimated £500,000 cost was well out of the budget of the Cornwall Railway.

The plans finally chosen were no less ground-breaking however. They were based around a pair of arched tubular girders, fastened to four cast-iron columns in the middle of the river, supporting by suspension a pair of 450ft spans which would carry a single-track railway from one side of the river to another. As with the Cornwall Railway main line, an early double-track blueprint had to be scaled back for reasons of economy.

Brunel's Tamar bridge was a development of his ground-breaking Usk bridge at Chepstow on the South Wales Railway. His choice of tubular steel was clearly inspired by its use in his much smaller and earlier swing bridge at the entrance to Bristol's Floating Harbour.

Test borings of the muddy riverbed were carried out on April 26, 1848, so Brunel could survey the rock strata, and an 85ft tall iron cylinder 6ft wide was sunk in 35 different places to allow 175 test borings to be made. Charles Mare, a shipbuilder from Blackwall who had built the ironwork for Robert Stephenson's Britannia Bridge over the Menai Straits, was in 1853 awarded the contract to build the Tamar bridge.

The piers on the Cornwall side were completed in 1854 and the girders hauled up into position; however, Mare went bankrupt on September 21, 1855, and on Brunel's recommendation the Cornwall Railway continued the work itself. Brunel's assistant Robert Pearson Brereton was appointed supervisor.

A huge wrought-iron cylinder was sunk in midstream after a highly complex and elaborate operation. Inside, workmen toiled away in nightmare conditions on the riverbed, digging down to the rock strata so that a solid granite column could be fixed in it. The column supports the cast-iron pillars which in turn hold the tubular arches.

The tubular girders were assembled on the east bank and weighed 1060 tons when finished. They were floated across the river into position on pontoons after a special dock was cut in the Devon bank. The Cornish span was jacked up with hydraulic presses in 3ft stages until it reached the required height, in an operation which drew large crowds after it began on September 1, 1857. The Devon span was floated into place on July 10, 1858, and was in its final position on December 28, 1858.

Attached to each tube were the suspension chains, linked to each other by 11 uprights. Diagonal bracing was added to provide extra rigidity.

The lower ties of the trusses were formed of chains made from 20ft links. Many had been obtained from the suspended works for Brunel's Clifton Suspension Bridge.

Brunel had accrued vast experience in lifting suspension bridges when he assisted in the construction of the Conway and Britannia bridges and this proved invaluable as the immensely difficult project progressed. The 730-yard bridge took seven years to build — even longer than Box Tunnel. Its £225,000 cost stretched the delicate finances of the Cornwall Railway to the limits, yet the directors were happy because they saw the clear rewards that it would bring.

They were able to make an inspection of their bridge by train on April 11, 1859. Nine days later, it underwent a statutory inspection and tests by Colonel Yolland on behalf of the Board of Trade, ran a heavy train across and measured deflections of 1.14in the Devon truss, and 1.2in in the Cornwall one. He came to the conclusion that the bridge was "highly satisfactory".

East of the Tamar bridge, the Cornwall Railway bought the South Devon's branch from Millbay to Devonport which had opened in 1849, and extended it. Millbay station was expanded to cope with the anticipated rise in traffic.

By the time the bridge had been built, the railway from Truro had been completed. On May 2 it was formally opened by the Prince Consort, hence its name: the Royal Albert Bridge. Both banks of the river were packed with onlookers while an armada of steamers and small boats enjoyed a closer view from the river itself.

Despite its mineral wealth and mining industry, Cornwall was up to that point the last remaining county in England without a railway connection. The mayors of Truro and Penzance arrived by train and were presented to the prince. A grand civic banquet was held in the town hall at Truro the next day. Guests arrived on a special train which left Plymouth at 10.30am and arrived just before 1pm. Everyone living in towns and villages along the railway cheered the train as it passed. Two days later, the railway opened throughout to the public.

Isambard was missing from all of these proceedings however, because by now his health was failing fast. He did see his magnificent bridge though, taking a ride over it on a couch mounted on a truck a few days later, the train being pulled by a Daniel Gooch-designed locomotive.

THE DEATH OF BRUNEL

Shortly after the Great Western Steamship Company had been wound up in 1852, Isambard began drawing up plans for an even bigger steamship nearly twice the size of the SS *Great Britain*, as described in Chapter 8.

The effort of building the ship, which was eventually named the SS *Great Eastern*, and the financial losses incurred in doing so took their toll on the workaholic Brunel, who allowed his health to deteriorate. He and his wife Mary took a holiday in Switzerland in a bid to recuperate in May 1858, but they did not return home until the autumn.

Despite being diagnosed with a kidney problem, Isambard did not hesitate in accepting the post of engineer to the Great Ship Company, which took over the building of the ship from the Eastern Steam Navigation Company.

He spent that winter on convalescence in the Mediterranean, and even met Robert Stephenson in Cairo. However, with his illness having been only too clear at the time of the opening of the Royal Albert Bridge, he then failed to show up at a celebratory banquet held to mark the completion of the SS *Great Eastern* on August 5, 1859.

He wanted so badly to go on the maiden voyage, and visited the ship on September 2, but after two hours he collapsed and had to be taken home. He was dying.

The maiden voyage began on September 7, but Isambard was confined to bed in his Duke Street home and had to be content with receiving news of his ship, which brought out the crowds as it passed every south coast town on its voyage from London to Holyhead.

He even wrote to the Great Western Railway directors, asking them to give all the workers at Swindon the day off along with special passes so they could ride to Weymouth by train and see his ship when it arrived. It was to be his last letter.

Around 6pm on September 8, as the SS *Great Eastern* passed Dungeness, there was a huge explosion on board which sent the forward funnel flying 30ft into the air along with a huge cloud of smoke and steam. Five stokers were killed and others seriously injured. A stopcock on a water pre-heater on the funnel had been left shut by mistake, resulting in a build-up of pressure.

Nonetheless, the ship continued her voyage, arriving in Weymouth as planned on September 10. Isambard was told about the tragedy that same day and was understandably horrified. Five days later, he called his family together for the last time and died a few hours later, aged just 53.

His funeral, attended by a large contingent of GWR staff, took place at Kensal Green Cemetery in London on September 20, 1859. He was laid to rest in the same tomb as his mother and father.

The words 'I.K. BRUNEL, ENGINEER, 1859' appear in large metal letters on either end of the Royal Albert Bridge, added as a memorial after his death.

BRUNEL'S BIG RAILWAY REACHES PENZANCE

The final part of the original Cornwall Railway route, from Truro to Falmouth, was not opened until August 23, 1863. The opening of new docks at Falmouth in 1861 led to fresh calls for it to be finished, but by then the port had lost the Royal Mail Packet Service fleet which had switched to Southampton after more than 150 years. The knock-on effect was that the Falmouth extension would become merely a branch of a main line that would run all the way through to Penzance instead.

Before that could happen, however, there had to be uniformity of gauge – and the West Cornwall Railway was built to 4ft 8½in. Drawing on the powers given to build the West Cornwall in 1864, the broad gauge Cornwall Railway gave it notice that it was required to lay broad gauge rails throughout.

The West Cornwall could not afford to do so and decided to offer itself for sale. The consortium of the GWR, Bristol & Exeter and the South Devon railways stepped in, taking over the working of the line from July 1, 1865, before completing the purchase on New Year's Day 1866.

The broad gauge rails were then laid west of Truro, creating mixed gauge. The first broad gauge freight trains ran on November 6, 1866, with passenger services beginning on March 1 the following year. There were two through Paddington services each way from Penzance daily, the engine supplied by the South Devon Railway.

Paddington to Penzance: the phrase was to enter railway folklore, and the dream of Brunel and his GWR directors was finally realised. The broad gauge empire by now stretched north to Wolverhampton and westwards to Milford Haven and Penzance. However, narrow gauge trains continued to run over the West Cornwall, and after November 1871, some freight trains contained wagons of both gauges!

The consortium amalgamated as the Great Western Railway in 1876, with the West Cornwall system becoming part of that company. Much had to be done to improve the infrastructure. Brunel's timber trestle viaducts were replaced by masonry and/or iron versions during 1885-88, apart from the one at Penzance. It was all but washed away on New Year's Eve 1868, and a replacement was opened on October 28, 1871.

CHAPTER FIFTEEN

Defeat!

ITH WORLD record timings for passenger trains and bigger
payloads, on paper Brunel's broad gauge should have set the
standard for railways everywhere. However, from the outset
it was doomed to fail.

As far back as the passing of the GWR's enabling Act in 1835, when
Brunel had the gauge omitted from the parliamentary bill, he would have
known that there was the strong possibility, probably a certainty, that
there would arise a clash with adjoining railways that had been built to
standard gauge.

His empire was not just Paddington to Penzance, but a myriad of other
railways and routes that linked with the GWR main line – the South Wales
Railway route to Milford Haven, Swindon to Cheltenham and Gloucester,
Paddington to Wolverhampton via Birmingham Snow Hill, Paddington
via Reading and Westbury to Weymouth, to name but a few.

Broad and standard (then called narrow) gauge tracks first met at
Gloucester in 1844, when the 7ft 0¼in gauge Bristol & Gloucester Railway
entered Gloucester to terminate at a temporary station on the north side
of the 4ft 8½in gauge Birmingham & Gloucester Railway terminus. Freight
workings began through Gloucester that September, and immediately

the break of gauge made its presence known. Most through traffic was for Birmingham, and goods had to be literally manhandled from one train to another.

The railway had been a great benefactor and liberator to society, but now it was becoming restrictive. Wherein lay the logic or gain of having to transfer passengers and freight from one train to another to make a cross-country journey, just because one company's train cannot run on the other company's tracks?

Lack of standardisation has probably beset the human race since the dawn of technology. In the households of our modern world, it readily manifests itself in the fact that one person's mobile telephone, laptop or iPad charger will not charge another's telephone, laptop or iPad. The author himself has remained loyal to the Pentax brand of camera since the firm's screw-thread lens days, because changing to Canon or Nikon would mean discarding a superb collection of lenses which fit only the Pentax K and its later derivatives.

The gauge controversy grew in parallel to that of the national rail network, and in 1845, just 10 years after the GWR was given its royal assent, a Gauge Commission was established by the Government to decide which was the best way forward for Britain.

Trials were held between two standard gauge engines and Gooch's Firefly class *Ixion* — which recorded superior performances despite using less coke and water. By contrast, one of its competitors was North Midland Railway No. 54 *Stephenson* which ran off the line and toppled over after just 22 miles.

The commissioners were faced with claims that while broad gauge track was cheaper to build, it cost more to repair. Gooch showed that while his locomotives were more expensive to build, they cost less to repair. Often, two standard gauge engines were needed to pull a train, whereas a similar load on the broad gauge needed just one.

What settled the issue — and left many historians wondering why trials were held at all — was the proliferation of standard gauge lines. At that stage, there were 1901 miles of standard gauge railway routes but just 274 miles of 7ft 0¼in broad gauge. Widening the standard gauge would involve phenomenally expensive rebuilding of infrastructure, especially with tunnels — while it would present far fewer difficulties to narrow the broad gauge.

Brunel challenged the findings of the Gauge Commission and managed to win some breathing space for the broad gauge. An Act for regulating the Gauge of Railways received royal assent on August 18, 1846. It stipulated that all future railways in Great Britain should be 4ft 8½in or 5ft 3in in Ireland, unless a specific exception was made, but it did not order the GWR to narrow itself at that moment.

The broad gauge pushed on to Wolverhampton via Oxford and was poised for expansion to the Mersey and the heartland of Bristol's old rival Liverpool, but was blocked through political manoeuvring by London & North Western Railway manager Captain Mark Huish, which forced the GWR to lay a third rail for standard gauge on some of its lines.

The GWR built its first standard gauge engines in 1855, a year after absorbing its first 4ft 8½in lines with the Shrewsbury & Chester and Shrewsbury & Birmingham railways. As more standard gauge railway companies amalgamated, especially in South Wales where there were 30 breaks of gauge impeding the lucrative coal traffic, the GWR had to convert more of its broad gauge system to mixed gauge.

The third rail reached the holy of holies of the broad system, Paddington, in August 1861. Gooch became GWR chairman in 1865, and by then he knew that the broad gauge had lost the battle. He drew up plans to convert large areas of broad gauge to standard. The following year, the first such conversions took place and by 1869, broad gauge trains no longer ran north of Oxford.

The last broad gauge train in Wales ran in 1872. Around 200 miles of branches south of the main line in Berkshire, Wiltshire, Hampshire and Somerset were converted by the end of 1873. All broad gauge carriages built from 1877 onwards were convertible to standard gauge.

Broad gauge lines were still being built, notably the first 3¾-mile section of the Metropolitan Railway which opened to the public on Saturday, January 10, 1863, with stations at Bishop's Road (now Paddington), Edgware Road, Baker Street, Portland Road (now Great Portland Street), Gower

Street (now Euston Square), King's Cross (now King's Cross St Pancras) and Farringdon Street (now Farringdon).

The railway carried 38,000 passengers on its opening day, using Great Northern Railway trains to supplement the service, as it was laid to mixed gauge. In the first 12 months, 9.5 million passengers were carried, and in the second year this soared to 12 million. A global first, the Metropolitan Railway was the blueprint for other major cities around the world to build underground railways.

Motive power was provided by GWR Metropolitan class broad gauge 2-4-0Ts fitted with condensing apparatus for working trains in the tunnels.

However, soon after opening there was a dispute with the GWR over the need to increase the service frequency. The GWR pulled out in August 1863, withdrawing its stock, leaving the GNR providing replacements until the Met could build its own.

The last passenger line built to broad gauge was the St Ives branch which opened on June 1, 1877, while an extension to the freight-only Sutton Harbour line in Plymouth was built to broad gauge and opened two years later.

Gooch died in 1889, leaving behind him Brunel's Big Railway, still in its original form. All 177 miles from Paddington to Bristol; Exeter, Plymouth and Penzance were still broad gauge. But it had to go. With the pruning of the broad gauge network, there had been little investment in new locomotives, apart from 'convertibles', which could be altered to run on either gauge, and carriages to run over it. The last broad gauge engine built at Swindon, Rover class 4-2-2 No. 24 *Tornado*, was outshopped in July 1888.

Like the last snow on an early spring day, the broad gauge would be washed away overnight — the GWR made the decision in February 1891. The final conversion of gauge was planned in minute detail, almost down to the last rail fastener. Paddington's general manager issued a 50-page manual of instructions, accompanied by a further 30 pages for the superintendents of the Bristol and Exeter divisions.

Before the big day, or night rather, ballast was cleared, facing points and complex crossovers made up on site in advance, nuts and tie-bolts oiled and freed, new rails and every third sleeper or transom on existing track measured and cut. Standard gauge locomotives were shipped to strategic locations on the route, carried on broad gauge trucks.

The last broad gauge train from Paddington to Penzance departed on Friday, May 20, at 10.15am, hauled appropriately by Great Western. It reached the Cornish terminus at 8.20pm and set off back to Swindon 50 minutes later, collecting redundant broad gauge stock with it.

The two last Up and Down broad gauge trains actually passed each other at Dawlish station that evening. When the trains arrived, the passengers pulled down their windows and shook hands with each other and sang the chorus of Auld Lang Syne. The final broad gauge passenger train of all over Brunel's Big Railway was hauled by 1880-built Rover class *Bulkeley*. It left Paddington at 5pm on May 20 for Temple Meads, returning early the following day with the last train from Penzance, the 'Night Mail'. The name *Bulkeley* honoured a longstanding GWR director.

The last broad gauge train from Penzance was a 9.10pm empty stock working, hauled by a pair of convertibles which would find use on the new standard gauge system.

As the last broad gauge train passed through each station on its one-way eastbound journey to oblivion, the stationmaster had to confirm to the inspector aboard that there was no broad gauge stock left in his sidings. The inspector then presented him with a certificate to be handed over to the line engineer as the signal to begin the conversion.

At daybreak on Saturday, May 21, 1892, 4200 platelayers and gangers assembled along the Paddington to Penzance line, all set to work through-out the night on the gauge conversion. It was a massive civil engineering operation, of which Brunel, bizarrely, just might have been proud. All broad gauge rolling stock and non-essential engines had already been taken back to Swindon, filling 15 miles of temporary sidings with a massive fleet of engines, carriages and wagons that would never run again. A total of 196 locomotives, 347 coaches and 3544 wagons survived to the end.

Such was the speed of conversion that the first Down standard gauge test train reached Dawlish at 1.15pm that day. The Up line was finished at 6pm on the Sunday.

The St Ives branch was also converted that weekend.

THE END OF THE BIG RAILWAY

On May 22, *The Times'* special correspondent wrote:

"The death of the broad gauge is the question on which the public attention of the West of England is riveted at the present moment. The inspectors and other officials of the Great Western, for whom lodgings have been found in cottages along the line, report that the inhabitants treat them as though they were soldiers returning from a victorious campaign.

Crowds remained round the stations on Friday night watching the departure of the various empty trains, and crowds are watching this morning the first signs of the resumption of the interrupted traffic. I left Millbay station at about half-past one on Saturday morning in a train of empty coaches, and there was still quite a crowd on the platform as a salute of fog signals announced the final closing of that station, and there were still 50 or 100 people watching North Road station when an hour later the 'Cornishman' came in from Penzance. The inspector, after delivering his notice to the stationmaster that the last broad gauge vehicle was through, got in and the Cornishman went off over the hills to Totnes, carrying the same message to every station as it passed. By 5 o'clock there was not a broad gauge vehicle left west of Exeter.

But an hour before this the engineer's staff were hard at work on the permanent way all the way from Newton Abbot and Falmouth. The London mail came down from Exeter on the Southwestern line, and the Cornish portion was transferred at once from the train at North Road to the docks at Millbay, where the Gazelle, *one of the fast new boats that work the Great Western service between Weymouth and Jersey, was in waiting to receive it. The mail was, I was told, less in bulk than usual, as Plymouth had taken the precaution of sending on all that was ready before the line was closed, but even so the waist of the steamer was piled up high with the huge parcel post hampers.*

We reached Fowey, where I left the steamer at about 7 o'clock and found the population of the place lining the shore and two four-horse omnibuses ready to take on the mails to Bodmin and St Austell. The steamer went on to Falmouth, where the remaining mails were landed and sent on by coach to Truro, whence the narrow gauge line was open all the way to Penzance.

From Fowey I went by another narrow gauge line to Par and then walked up the main Cornwall line for some eight miles to Bodmin Junction. All the way the scene was a busy one — the station yards were alive with men and even between the stations one came on groups of men every hundred yards or so. At one point it was the cook in charge of the thin oatmeal gruel which the company keep flowing all day in a perennial stream; at another men were sawing off the end of the transoms.

A gang of ten or a dozen men, each armed with a gigantic crowbar, stationed themselves two feet apart along a length of rail, and with a series of rhythmic lifts and heaves lifted the line of longitudinals, with the rails on the top of them, six or eight inches inwards; then moved on another eight or 10 yards and repeated the process, and so on till they got to the end of their stretch of line. Then, returning, they would in similar fashion close up another six or eight inches, till finally, with a third lift, the two rails would arrive at the proper narrow gauge distance apart.

As long as the road was perfectly straight, the work was, comparatively speaking, of a simple nature, so much so that at midday I found an entire stretch of a mile that at a cursory glance seemed perfectly finished.

I might have said much of the clearing up at Millbay station on Friday night; of drivers of broad gauge engines wandering disconsolably about with their engine lamps in their hands, followed by their firemen, with pick and shovel over the shoulder, waiting in anxious expectation of the time when that new-fangled machine, a narrow gauge engine, would come down a day or two after and they would have to 'go to school' again, with different machinery and different fireboxes. I might have pointed out that the population of Devonshire must have been much understated in the census returns, to judge by the fact that the hedges and bridges all along the line have been crowded with eager gazers all day today. Or, again, I might enlarge on the benefits the west of England is likely to derive from the even uniformity of gauge.

Already it is announced that from June 1 there will be a through express every day between Torquay and Liverpool, and that the historic 'Dutchman' is to be henceforth divided into two. But I must forbear, and will conclude in the words which I found written on one of the rails: 'Goodbye, poor old broad gauge, God bless you'.

Through the liberality of Mr Wills of Bristol, one of the directors of the Great Western Railway, 5000 men employed in making the alterations were each served with 2oz of tobacco."

The conversion was completed early on the morning of Monday, May 23, allowing for 'normal' standard gauge services to operate from then on. The mail train from Penzance to Paddington which departed Plymouth at 4.40am that day was the first to run the length of the new all-standard gauge GWR main line. In less than two days, 56 years of history had finally been eradicated.

The last GWR broad gauge engines to steam were South Devon Railway 4-4-0STs *Leopard* and *Stag*, which were pressed into service at Swindon for shunting the redundant 7ft 0¼in gauge stock into the cutting shop for scrapping. In June 1893, they met the same fate.

THE FINAL VERDICT FROM 1892

The Times summed up much of the debate about Brunel's broad gauge in its leader on May 23:

"The broad gauge is no more. Today marks its final extinction and the triumph of its old rival, the narrow gauge. The letter which we publish this morning from our Special Correspondent (above) *tells us in detail how the change has been carried out in the last three days.*

We record the fact with mixed feelings. Of the necessity of the change we have no doubt. Uniformity of gauge is of the first importance in a country crossed and re-crossed in every direction by networks of lines, which are of use to one another and to the public in just the degree in which they can be combined to form one harmonious whole.

A line which stands out from the rest by the adoption of a different gauge can neither give nor receive the amenities of an interchange of accommodation. It thus causes a breach of continuity where continuity would be of essential service, and if it persists in its policy of isolation it must do so at no small cost to itself and to its disobliged neighbours.

This policy the Great Western Railway has at length finally given up, and the longstanding battle of the gauges is at an end. But the disappearance of the broad gauge is an event which we record with some regret and with some sense of loss. It is a triumph of utility, of common sense, of convenience; it is a concession to an irresistible foe; it has been long inevitable and it has come now as sooner or later it must have come. But the change thus made is by no means an unmixed benefit.

The broad gauge had something more than a sentimental claim on our regard. It was a comfortable gauge to travel by. It allowed with safety a higher speed than can be attained by its rival. An express train on the old Great Western line conveyed its inmates not only more rapidly but more smoothly than almost any other line in the country.

The line, we must admit, cost more in construction; it was worked at greater expense. From the shareholders' point of view there can be no doubt which of the two systems was preferable. But its great champion, Brunel, had a soul above such base monetary considerations.

His mind was in the grand style, and such too must be his work. But the views which found favour with him did not therefore commend themselves to intelligences cast in a different mould.

His triumphs consequently were limited to the sphere within which he ruled supreme. There and there only could he give play to his inventive powers.

On all sides of him another spirit prevailed, and another system was set up. His position thus became untenable, long and stoutly as he refused to recognise the fact.

The battle of Athanasius Contra Mundum may be carried on with success in the superlunar regions of theology. In the workaday world of common life, the one must yield to the many.

So it has been the case with the broad gauge, and given the facts of the case, we could not wish that it had been otherwise. Our regret is not that the weaker system has succumbed to the stronger, but rather that the chapter of accidents has turned out unhappily for it, and that by becoming the weaker, it has thus been forced to succumb.

It had good prospects once, and good chances of success. The uniformity of gauge, which has been secured by its disappearance, would have been equally well served by its general adoption. But the fates and the Stephensons have ruled the matter otherwise, and while we accept the result, we cannot refuse to give our hearty endorsement to the concluding words with which our Correspondent's letter of today dismisses the broad gauge into the great limbo of nonentity.

The issue of the battle of the gauges has been certain for some time past, and it has ended now in the way which has been long foreseen by railway experts and by the public. The narrow gauge has been the successfully aggressive power.

On some branches of the Great Western Railway it was not in use at all times. Elsewhere, and most notably on the main line, it had its place allowed side by side with the broad gauge, and having thus crept into recognition, it has now, cuckoo-like, dispossessed the original occupant and has taken the Great Western Railway all through as its own.

It has been a wise course on the part of the directors to complete the process of transformation which their line has been undergoing by degrees. Its full benefit will not be felt immediately, but it will come in due course and in all probability after no very long delay.

The Great Western has recently been a decidedly progressive line. Its stock stands already among the highest in the heavy railway market, and we may expect it to improve under the stimulus of the new traffic which it may henceforth look to receive. Its territory, for which it has fought hard, and which it has not been able to keep entirely as its own, is a valuable one, capable of development in all directions.

What great expectations are entertained in the West of England as to the results to follow from the change which is completed today, we may judge from the interest with which the work has been watched, and from the hearty welcome given to those who have been instrumental in carrying it through.

It has been anxious work for the railway authorities and very hard work for the labourers. Our Correspondent describes exactly the process, the difficulties which have attended it and the pluck and energy which have triumphed over all difficulties.

His letter does justice to the thoroughness of English workmanship as tested by actual use. The operations on the line between Exeter and Truro, where the change of gauge has been made, have displayed to the public on a large scale the nature of railway construction everywhere.

The broad gauge has much that can be said for it, and much that might have been said for it in its old days while the contest was as yet undecided.

That it has disappeared has been in compliant with the harsh law of the survival only of the fittest. Its chief appeal has thus come to be to sentiment, and in the world of affairs sentiment must give way to use.

Like the old paddle steamer, it has been displaced by a new rival, and like the old paddle steamer it will be regretted by those who have a grateful memory of the convenience and comfort and easy travelling which they enjoyed in days which are now no more, and which can never be expected to return."

Brunel's broad gauge won many arguments and battles, but lost the war. However, *The Times'* leader writer was not far off the mark regarding his prediction for the fortunes of the new standard gauge GWR, which was to win many, many victories in the century that followed, and carry on in the Brunel tradition and spirit if not the physical reality at track level.

CHAPTER SIXTEEN

Clifton Suspension Bridge: Brunel's 'bookends'

W HAT BETTER monument could you have to one of the world's greatest engineering geniuses than to turn one of his designs into reality? Clifton Suspension Bridge is the ultimate tribute to a man who inspired a planet.

Work on turning Isambard Kingdom Brunel's design for the colossal landmark bridge across the limestone Avon Gorge, down which his first great steamships had set off on their maiden voyages, began in 1831, but floundered due to the Bristol Riots that year, and was stalled for decades because of a lack of investment to complete the project.

The work resumed only in the years following Isambard's death, and was completed in 1864 mainly as a tribute to him. The decades between the start and completion of the bridge, arguably Bristol's most internationally recognised landmark, encompassed Brunel's ground-breaking career, including the building of the Great Western Railway main line. It marked, in effect, the start and end of his great works and might therefore be viewed as 'bookends' on Brunel's illustrious career, which is sandwiched between those dates.

The bridge project was not killed off by the riots. After the Great Western Railway Act was passed, commercial confidence flowed once more through Bristol's streets.

Work began again in 1836, but the main contractors went bankrupt the following year, leaving the towers unfinished. A 1000ft-long iron bar was installed between the two towers, allowing for the transfer of building materials between the two.

Finance ran out again in 1843, and with a shortfall of £30,000, all work stopped. The project had also overrun its time limit as stipulated in its Act of Parliament. Brunel came up with the idea of building a deepwater port at Portbury — visionary indeed, for this was not done until the 1970s — with a view to making the bridge an essential line of communication.

In 1851, the ironwork was sold and reused on Brunel's Royal Albert Bridge at Saltash. The Clifton towers, however, were left in place. Today's health and safety gurus would be horrified by what happened next: the iron bar that had been installed as an aid to construction was used to carry passengers in a basket slung beneath it!

Brunel died in 1859 and never saw the bridge completed; indeed, he may well have given up all hope of ever doing so. That was sad, because it was his bridge design which helped set about a chain of events which led to his appointment as engineer of the GWR. Brunel's compatriots in the Institution of Civil Engineers felt much the same. They wanted to see it completed as a memorial to him, and set about raising new funds. In 1860 the Clifton Bridge Company was set up to oversee the final stages of completion.

As luck would have it, Brunel's Hungerford suspension bridge over the Thames in London was demolished in 1860 to make way for a new railway bridge to Charing Cross station. The Clifton project revivalists bought the chains.

Two of mid-Victorian Britain's great railway civil engineers, William Henry Barlow and Sir John Hawkshaw, then made slight revisions to Brunel's design. As mentioned earlier, Barlow was engineer for the Midland Railway on its London extension and designed St Pancras station.

After the Tay Bridge disaster of December 28, 1879, when the central section of the North British Railway's bridge collapsed as an express train crossed it in a heavy storm, leaving 75 passengers and crew dead, Barlow led the design of the replacement.

Hawkshaw became chief engineer to the Manchester & Leeds Railway in 1845, and two years later was appointed to the same role at its successor, the Lancashire & Yorkshire Railway. Later, he was responsible for the railways serving Charing Cross and Cannon Street in London, along with the bridges that carried them over the Thames into the stations, and also engineered the East London Railway... which used Sir Marc Brunel's Thames Tunnel. Jointly with Sir J Wolfe-Barry, Henshaw constructed the section of the Underground which completed the inner circle between the Aldgate and Mansion House stations.

The pair's revisions included a wider, higher and sturdier deck than Brunel intended, with triple chains instead of double.

It was decided not to go to the expense of finishing the towers in the Egyptian style as Brunel proposed, for reasons of cost. So the towers remained in rough stone. Sufficient funds were finally raised to restart work on the bridge in 1862.

The first task was to replace the iron bar with a temporary bridge, made by hauling ropes across the gorge to create a footway of wire ropes with wood planks held together with iron hoops.

A 'traveller' was constructed to run over this temporary bridge, it was made of a light frame on wheels to transport each link individually. The links were assembled to make up the chains supporting the bridge. The chains were anchored in tapering tunnels, 82ft long, on either side of the bridge. Staffordshire blue brick was used to create plugs to stop the chains being pulled out of the narrower tunnel mouth.

When the chains were completed, vertical suspension rods were hung from the links in the chains and large girders hung from these. The girders on either side then supported the deck, which stood 3ft higher at the Clifton end than at Leigh Woods in order to create the impression of being horizontal.

Although similar in size, the bridge towers were not identical in design, the Clifton tower having side cut-outs and the Leigh Woods tower more pointed arches on top of a 110ft red sandstone clad abutment. In 2002, it was discovered that the Leigh Woods tower was not a solid structure as had always been thought, but contained 12 vaulted chambers up to 35ft high, connected by a series of shafts and tunnels.

Roller-mounted 'saddles' on top of each tower permit movement of the three independent wrought iron chains on each side when loads pass over the bridge. Although their total travel is minuscule, their ability to absorb forces created by chain deflection prevents damage to both tower and chain.

The bridge deck is suspended by 81 matching vertical wrought-iron rods.

Two men were apparently killed during construction work on the bridge. The fact was reported by Barlow himself, but nobody knows who they were or how the tragedies occurred.

After completion, the bridge had to be tested. A load of 500 tons of stone was spread over the bridge, causing it to sag by seven inches. However, that was well within safety tolerance levels.

The bridge was then deemed safe to use. On December 8, 1864, a ceremonial parade was held to mark its official opening, but high winds dampened the great occasion by blowing out the magnesium flares which had been lit to illuminate its profile.

In 1885, local girl Sarah Ann Henley was so distressed following an argument with her boyfriend that she jumped off the bridge. Famously, she was saved by her crinoline petticoats, which slowed her fall and cushioned the impact on the glistening low-tide mudflats below. Lucky Sarah was pulled alive from the mud and although injured, made a full recovery and lived until 1948 when she was 84.

The structure has since gained a reputation as a suicide bridge, and now carries plaques advertising the telephone number of the Samaritans. Anti-climb barriers have been fixed above the railings on the bridge.

On April 1, 1979, members of the University of Oxford Dangerous Sports Club made the first bungee jumps from the bridge. The practice is now banned at the bridge, although for the past decade it has been the scene of the modern-day pastime of base jumping, where participants jump from fixed objects as opposed to aircraft and use a parachute to break their fall. BASE is the acronym that stands for four categories of fixed objects from which participants jump – Buildings, Antennas, Spans (bridges) and Earth, for example, cliffs. On each occasion when base jumping has taken place from the bridge, the police have been called.

Until the 1930s, pilots occasionally flew beneath the bridge in biplanes. It is said that faster aircraft made the daredevil practice dangerous, although there are unconfirmed tales of Spitfires and others were flown underneath the deck during the Second World War. In 1957, Flying Officer Crossley of the RAF's 501 Squadron defied a ban on such flights and flew a Vampire Jet at 450mph from east to west under the bridge. He crashed into Leigh Woods and died instantly. In 1997, a police helicopter flew beneath the bridge during a search.

On November 26, 2003, the last ever Concorde flight (Concorde 216) flew over the bridge before landing at the city's Filton Aerodrome. Isambard would have been impressed to see that it would have been possible to extend his railway to New York with a mode of transport that would have taken just four hours instead of many days by his best steamship, but maybe saddened and even angry at Britain's decision to pull back from supersonic commercial flights.

Brunel designed his bridge long before the advent of motor traffic, but nonetheless it can still cope. The limit for vehicles is two and a half tons axle weight or four tons gross weight. Only motor cars, personnel carriers and small goods vehicles may cross, and the number of vehicles on the deck at any one time is effectively controlled by the toll barriers. Weighbridges are set into the road on both approaches to the bridge.

In 2003 and 2004, the volume of crowds travelling to and from the Ashton Court Festival and Bristol International Balloon Fiesta placed such great strain on the structure that it was decided to close it to all traffic and pedestrians for the duration of the events. Since then, it has been closed during all major events.

Celebrations to mark the bicentenary of Isambard's birth in 2006 saw the bridge illuminated by fireworks on April 8 during a centrepiece Brunel 200 weekend, which also involved the official switch-on of a state-of-the-art LED-based lighting array to illuminate the bridge — a far cry from the magnesium flares of 1864.

The bridge is now managed by the Clifton Suspension Bridge Trust, a non profit-making registered charity originally formed by the Society of Merchant Venturers following William Vick's bequest, as outlined in Chapter 2. On the top of the pier on the Leigh Woods side is the Latin inscription SUSPENSA VIX VIA FIT, meaning "the road becomes barely suspended", and the 'Vix' is held to be a pun on Vick.

The trust was authorised to manage the bridge and collect tolls by Acts of Parliament in 1952, 1980 and 1986. The tolls are used to pay for the upkeep of the bridge including the strengthening of the chain anchor points in 1925 and 1939 and regular painting and maintenance. The trust's only source of revenue is the tolls.

There are 12 unpaid trustees, who between them have a range of expertise, particularly in engineering. Ten of them are local residents and two are representatives of Bristol City Council and North Somerset Council. The Bridgemaster, a fully qualified civil engineer, is responsible for the everyday running of the bridge.

May 23, 2012, saw the London 2012 Olympic Torch relay cross the bridge, with two of the torchbearers exchanging the flame in the middle. In December that year, the Heritage Lottery Fund awarded £595,000 for a new Clifton Suspension Bridge Heritage and Learning Centre to be built on the Leigh Woods side, allowing the Clifton Suspension Bridge Trust to open up the bridge's unique history to a much wider audience in time for the 150th anniversary of the bridge's completion in 2014. A new learning centre will provide space for schools and community groups.

Downstream from the bridge, on the Somerset short of the Severn estuary, is another classic structure with links to Isambard, even though he played no part whatsoever in its design and construction and would have had no knowledge of it whatsoever.

The agricultural village of Clevedon took off as a seaside resort in Victorian times after the Bristol & Exeter Railway opened a broad gauge branch from Yatton on the main line on July 28, 1847. In 1866, it was decided to build a pier at Clevedon so that pleasure steamers could call.

Its engineers, John Grover and Richard Ward, bought 37 tons of redundant Barlow rails which had been supplied to Brunel's South Wales Railway.

The rails were then bolted together almost like a giant Meccano set to form the legs of the elegant 1024ft eight-span pier which had to withstand the powerful currents of the Bristol Channel and its immense tidal range.

The pier was officially opened on March 29, 1869. It was described by the late Poet Laureate Sir John Betjeman as "the most beautiful pier in England" and given Grade I listed building protection in 2001, the only intact pier in Britain to have this status. It offers a landing stage for Bristol Channel steamers and remains a popular landmark for tourists.

'ULTIMATE' BRUNEL MUSEUM OPENS IN BRISTOL

The showpiece £7.2 million Being Brunel museum dedicated to the engineering genius who built the GWR opened its doors to the public on Bristol's Harbourside on March 23, 2018.

The new visitor attraction, next to the SS *Great Britain*, features six galleries setting out around 150 of Brunel's personal artefacts — many never seen in public before — to provide unprecedented insights into his life, family, interests and creative mind.

The new museum incorporates the historic Great Western Steamship Company's Dock Office, a Grade II* listed building where Brunel once worked, which has been restored as part of the project. Visitors can step and see where he designed the nearby steamship. Brunel's office was reconstructed based on a watercolour painted by his niece.

Exhibits include the opportunity to board a shaking 1830s broad-gauge carriage where 'passengers' will be able to compare their drawing skills to Brunel's while travelling. There is also a section of pipe from his short-lived South Devon atmospheric railway.

A wall-mounted regulator clock made by EJ Dent of London, which hung in Brunel's London office at 18 Duke Street, and which he set his watch by, has gone on public display for the first time. Regulator clocks were extremely reliable; and the reliability, speed and success of the GWR created the need for standardised timetabling, which ultimately contributed to the spread of Greenwich Mean Time across the UK.

The overall design evoked the atmosphere of the Great Exhibition of 1851 — which was a celebration of Victorian wonder and invention — and included Brunel on its design committee.

Arts, Heritage and Tourism Minister Michael Ellis said: "Being Brunel is a wonderful celebration of a British engineering great and an exceptional addition to Bristol's world-class heritage. I am delighted that £5.5 million from National Lottery players and the Government has made this possible. I am sure this exhibition will serve as an inspiration to many budding engineers and be a major draw for visitors from at home and abroad."

REDISCOVERED IN IRELAND

In 2019, a significant piece of railway engineering history in the form of a stone culvert built in the 1850s by Brunel was rediscovered as part of preparations for the Dunkettle Interchange Project to build a slip road on a motorway interchange near Cork in Ireland. It was constructed as part of the Cork & Youghal Railway and was said to be in excellent condition. The project team hailed it as "an admirable feat of engineering from 160 years ago."

The 5ft 3in gauge Cork & Youghal Railway obtained its Act of Parliament on July 31, 1854, and Brunel considered the project to be as an opportunity to extend the influence of the GWR into Ireland.

When Brunel died in 1859 he was succeeded there by Edward Cadwallader Edwards, who had been his resident engineer on the Cork & Youghal Railway and before that on the Oxford & Birmingham Railway.

CHAPTER SEVENTEEN

Slimmed down but still super fast!

ISAMBARD KINGDOM Brunel never lost the argument over the individual merits of his Big Railway. Instead, he was effectively shouted down so that nobody was listening to it any more. The railways shrunk the British Isles and then the world, in terms of mass communication.

On a comparatively small island, it was understandable that a national network should be of an uniform size, but did the best man win? Many believe that he didn't.

Harsh reality forced the GWR, more than three decades after Brunel's death, to abandon his broad gauge. However, the company was none the worse for it, and its routes and infrastructure, much of which dated from the Brunel era, reached new dizzier heights.

In 1886, it opened the four-mile 624-yard Severn Tunnel, which for more than a century was the longest main line railway tunnel in the UK, until the London East and West tunnels opened in 2007 as part of the High Speed 1 channel tunnel rail link.

After 1892, relieved of the burden of operating trains on two gauges, the company diverted its resources to constructing new lines and upgrading old ones to reduce the old circuitous routes. In 1903, the South Wales and Bristol Direct Railway from Wootton Bassett was opened to link up with the Severn Tunnel. The following year, the Cornwall Railway route between Saltash and St Germans was diverted, eliminating the last wooden viaducts on the main line.

From 1906, the Langport and Castle Cary Railway shortened the journey from London to Penzance between Reading and Taunton. Three years later, a new route was built linking Birmingham via Stratford-upon-Avon to Cheltenham, giving fresh access to the coalfields of South Wales. Part of it is now restored as the Gloucestershire Warwickshire Railway.

At the same time, the lot of the GWR passenger consistently improved, with new faster expresses, restaurant cars, better conditions for third class passengers and steam heating of trains. The GWR ran its first corridor train, from Paddington to Birkenhead, on October 1, 1892, and the next year, some of its trains were for the first time heated by steam passed through the carriages in a pipe from the locomotive.

In May 1896, first-class restaurant cars were introduced, and the service was expanded to cater for all classes in 1903. Sleeping cars for third-class passengers between Paddington and Penzance became available in 1928.

Chief mechanical engineer George Jackson Churchward is credited with producing the first 'modern' GWR locomotive types. On May 9, 1904, one of the 10-strong City class of 4-4-0s, No. 3440 *City of Truro*, was unofficially recorded as having hit 102.3mph with the 'Ocean Mails Special' on Wellington Bank in Somerset. Brunel and Gooch no doubt would have been impressed.

Churchward's successor, Charles B Collett, took over two years before the GWR absorbed 27 smaller companies and their constituents at the Grouping of 1923, which came about as a result of the Railways Act 1921. He was charged with providing a fleet to operate a much-expanded system, and replaced old locomotive types along with those inherited from the smaller concerns with new standard designs.

He was no Gooch, designing straight off the drawing board, but modified many of Churchward's designs and ideas. Collett's best-known and greatest successes were the Castle and then the King 4-6-0s, which became bywords for cutting edge locomotive technology of the day.

One legacy of the broad gauge was that trains for certain routes could be constructed slightly wider than normal in Britain. Such carriages included the 1929-built 'Super Saloons' for the boat train services which took transatlantic passengers to London in luxury. When the GWR celebrated its centenary in 1935, new 'Centenary' carriages were built for the 'Cornish Riviera Express', again making full use of the wider loading gauge on the Paddington to Penzance route. Broad gauge passed into history, but Big Railway had not gone away, and the rich old wine was decanted into new bottles.

BEATING THE WORLD YET AGAIN

On June 6, 1932, the 'Cheltenham Spa Express', nicknamed the 'Cheltenham Flyer', broke railway speed records with a time of 56 minutes 47 seconds at an average speed of 81.6mph over the 77¼ miles between Swindon and Paddington.

The century before, the Bristol & Exeter had been the fastest railway in the world: now the Swindon empire had regained the mantle. For this run, the 'Flyer' was hauled by No. 5006 *Tregenna Castle* and was crewed by driver Harry Rudduck and fireman Thorp of Old Oak Common shed. The tender survives in preservation today, at the Northampton & Lamport Railway.

In September 1932, the timings from Swindon to London were cut to 65 minutes, with an average speed, for the time, of 71.3mph. It was the first time in railway history that any train had been scheduled at over 70mph.

The improvement in social conditions and regular holidays for workers brought big dividends for Brunel's big route to the west, which in the age before the car became king, was the principal means of ordinary families to reach seaside resorts.

Nationalisation on January 1, 1948, following years of wartime austerity in which Britain's railways run down, saw the GWR become the Western Region of British Railways. Old rivalries were meant to disappear with the wave of a hand, in a new one-size-fits-all culture.

However, legislation cannot force a leopard to change it spots, and the Paddington empire, just as in the defiant days of Brunel and the broad gauge, continued to go its own way. Members of the GWR management had opposed the company's nationalisation into British Railways and although their hands were tied by Clement Attlee's Labour government, they did not go willingly.

GWR-design locomotives and rolling stock continued to be built for several years. Express trains were once again named and their carriages were painted in chocolate and cream between 1956-62, while stations carried the same livery.

The GWR may have been called the Western Region, but its old enmity with near neighbour the London, Midland & Scottish Railway continued unabated with its incarnation as the London Midland Region.

DAY OF THE DIESELS

In 1955, the British Railways Modernisation Plan ordered the replacement of steam locomotives with diesel and electric traction. The Western Region became the first part of British Railways to phase out steam — Isambard would have had no hesitation in doing the same if greater power and efficiencies could be proven — but again in typical Brunel fashion, did it by its own rules.

Whereas other regions opted for diesel-electric locomotives, the Western Region insisting on being different by choosing diesel hydraulic types instead. Indeed, a range of them covered the Type 1 to Type 4 power requirements. They included the Class 42 Warships, which were based on a West German design, and the successors to the Kings, the Maybach-engined Western Co-Cos, late Class 52s.

By the end of the Sixties, when British Rail insisted on greater standardisation of locomotive classes after several of the pioneer diesel types proved less satisfactory than the steam engines they had superseded, the diesel hydraulics were squeezed out, just as standard gauge had done with Brunel's broad gauge. Many were scrapped, others, the Class 14s shunters, found ready buyers in private industry. The last Westerns were withdrawn in 1977, the 'Western Tribute Railtour' from Paddington to Swansea and Bristol and back on February 26 in so many ways bringing down the curtain on Swindon's 'GWR' independence.

There were Western Region success stories. One was the introduction on the GWR main line of the Class 125 InterCity High Speed Train sets from 1976. From October that year, several were running 125 services, completely replacing locomotive-hauled trains on the Bristol and South Wales routes, and leading to sizeable increases in passenger numbers.

FAREWELL TO SWINDON WORKS

In February 1960, Swindon Works turned out its final steam locomotives for the home market, the last main line engine built for British Railways, in BR Standard 9F 2-10-0 No. 92220 *Evening Star*. Unlike other 9Fs which were not named, it was painted in the GWR livery of Brunswick green as well as a copper-capped double chimney and officially named at Swindon on March 18, 1960, when a special commemorative plaque was fixed to it.

The name was chosen in a competition run in 1959-60 by the BR Western Region staff magazine. *Evening Star* had been used twice before by GWR locomotives. *North Star* hauled the first GWR train, a sister engine was named *Morning Star*, and a later member of the same class was named *Evening Star*. Also, 1907-built Star 4-6-0 No. 4002 was named *Evening Star*.

No. 92220 is the only British main line steam locomotive earmarked for preservation from the time it was built, as the 999th British Railways Standard types built after nationalisation as a stopgap prior to dieselisation. It ran just five years in service prior to being withdrawn, and is now part of the National Collection.

A speech was given by R F Hanks, chairman of the Western Area Board of the British Transport Commission, in which he remarked: "I trust I shall not be considered parochial when I say that it is a proud day for Great Western men everywhere who will find much satisfaction, since there had to be a 'last one' that it should fall to the lot of Swindon to see the job through.

"I am sure it has been truly said that no other product of man's mind has ever exercised such a compelling hold upon the public's imagination as the steam locomotive. No other machine, in its day, has been a more faithful friend to mankind and has contributed more to the cause of industrial prosperity in this, the land of its birth, and throughout the world."

Brunel's great works had already been building diesels, and this continued up to 1965 with the short-lived Class 14 diesel-hydraulic shunters. Locomotive repairs and carriage and wagon work continued, though the original carriage and wagon workshop was sold.

British Rail Engineering Ltd closed Swindon Works in 1986, but part of it was revived by a series of small-scale heritage railway engineering businesses. The last locomotive left No. 9 Shop on May 2, 2007. It was not a GWR engine, but a humble Peckett saddle tank built in Bristol, which was restored in the guise of fictional children's book character, Ivor the Engine. The final GWR locomotive to leave was under-restoration ex-Barry scrapyard 2-8-2T No. 7200, representative of a type that has never steamed in preservation, and after the move was sponsored by *Heritage Railway* magazine, it is now being rebuilt at the Buckinghamshire Railway Centre.

Part of the works is now the McArthurGlen Designer Outlet Village retail park, while STEAM — Museum of the Great Western Railway has been established in a Grade II listed building on the works site.

ECHOES OF GREAT WESTERN GLORIES

The other big preservation site along Brunel's Big Railway is Didcot Railway Centre, next to Didcot Parkway station. Based around the former Didcot steam shed, it was taken over by the Great Western Society in 1967. Not only are there 20 GWR locomotives and a GWR diesel railcar on display alongside rolling stock, but it houses tens of thousands of artefacts ranging from the Burlescombe broad gauge transhipment shed and signalboxes to tickets.

The society also builds 'new' GWR locomotives. The replica *Fire Fly* runs on a broad gauge demonstration line at Didcot, and a new Churchward Saint 4-6-0, No. 2999 *Lady of Legend*, was completed in 2019. A new-build Hawksworth County 4-6-0, No. 1014 *County of Glamorgan* and Churchward 47XX mixed traffic 2-8-0 No. 4709 are also very much on the way.

The society also rebuilt GWR steam railmotor No. 93, building a new steam bogie to fit inside the surviving body, and its matching auto trailer No. 92. It plugged a major hole in railway heritage, providing a beautiful working example of a type of traction hugely successful on the GWR in Edwardian times, and forming the 'missing link' in the evolution of railways from steam haulage to diesel. And all of this in the shadow of the big railway that Brunel built.

The name Great Western lives on in regular main line service today. As part of the privatisation of British Rail in the early Nineties, Great Western was formed as a regional division prior to the franchise being let. The sector consisted of the express services out of Paddington to the West of England over Brunel's Big Railway to Bristol, Exeter and Penzance, and Cardiff and Swansea.

The holding company Great Western Holdings, which was part-owned by the Badgerline bus group, won the new Great Western franchise. Badgerline then became FirstGroup after merging with GRT Group, and in 1998 it bought Great Western Trains outright, rebranding it First Great Western. On April 1, 2006, the Great Western, Great Western Link and Wessex franchises were combined into a new Greater Western franchise, won by FirstGroup which kept the name First Great Western.

As with its steam era namesake, the company runs several named trains, including 'The Bristolian' (Paddington-Bristol), 'Cathedrals Express' (London-Hereford), 'Cheltenham Spa Express' (London-Cheltenham), the 'Cornish Riviera Express' (London-Penzance), 'The Golden Hind' (London-Penzance), 'The Mayflower' (London-Plymouth), 'Night Riviera' (London-Penzance sleeper), 'The Royal Duchy' (London-Penzance), 'The Atlantic Coast Express' (London-Newquay) and 'The Devon Express' (London-Paignton).

The value of the name coined for Isambard Kingdom Brunel's employer is clearly still currency today, and rightly so. It was a name of prestige, one that helped make Britain great in the eyes of the rest of the world at the height of its Commonwealth, leading the market with cutting-edge transport technology.

There have long been moves to make Brunel's original main line from Paddington to Bristol a World Heritage Site. Such recognition is long overdue, and listing by England Heritage of so many additional structures often overlooked by all but the most devout historians and enthusiasts will go a long way in boosting that cause.

Yet why not go much further — to the tune of 177 miles — and grant the status to the whole of the Paddington to Penzance route? It is the stuff of legend that still gives sterling service today.

Index

INDEX